Haunted Travels of Michigan

Volume II

Haunted Travels of Michigan

Volume II

History, Mystery & Haunting

Kathleen Tedsen & Beverlee Rydel

Thunder Bay Press

Holt, Michigan

www.hauntedtravelsMVG.com

Haunted Travels of Michigan, Volume II
by Kathleen Tedsen & Beverlee Rydel

Copyright © 2010
TR Desktop Publishing

All Rights Reserved

Published by
Thunder Bay Press
Holt, Michigan 48842

First Printing September 2010

15 14 13 12 11   10 9 8 7 6 5 4 3 2

ISBN: 978-1-933272-23-8

All photos taken by the authors except where credited.
Book and Cover design by Julie Taylor.
Front and Back cover photo with creative enhancement Beverlee Rydel and Kathleen Tedsen.

Printed in the United States of America
by McNaughton & Gunn, Inc.

Dedicated to the memory of

Christian E. Tedsen

His unconditional love and constant support made anything possible. He was a devoted husband, brother-in-law, and trusted friend. Kind, gentle and selfless ... there will never be another who can compare. His spirit will always be with us.

Wisdom tells me I am nothing
Love tells me I am everything
Between the two my life flows.
—Nisargadatta

Story Locations

1. Holly
2. Calumet
3. Jackson
4. Gulliver
5. Ann Arbor
6. Bay City
7. Lake
8. Clare
9. Flint
10. Allegan

Contents

Preface

These stories have been written in the first person to bring the reader into an investigation on a more personal level. Each story, however, has been a joint writing effort between the authors.

The authors' second book continues to break through the myths and legends to find the truth. Join them on their ghost hunts as they share firsthand accounts of the investigation and haunted history of each location, always with *a skeptic's eye.*

History plays an important part of each investigation. If past events or people can be tied in with the evidence collected, it makes the experience that much more rewarding. History tends to validate what is collected during an investigation.

The authors' experiences will sometimes be funny, sometimes thought-provoking and sometimes chilling. The stories and evidence revealed in this book and Web site will be true, unaltered and accurate. You'll see it and hear it just as we did (audio adjustments may be made for clarity). Ultimately, whether or not a location is haunted will be your decision.

Enjoy this book by itself or online for a complete interactive book/Web experience. You will be able to hear the electronic voice phenomenon (EVP), see up-close the unusual photographic and video evidence, listen to behind-the-scene activities, interviews and more as you follow along in the book.

The journey into the unknown continues.

Story Secret Rooms

How to Use Our Interactive Web site www.HauntedTravelsMI.com

To help bring you into each story, we have established a Web site, www.HauntedTravelsMI.com, with a "Secret Room" for each story. This Secret Room will include audio, video, and full color photographic evidence. It will also have some behind-the-scene video clips and/or photographs of what happened during the investigation.

Secret Rooms are Password Protected

Each story has a secret password that will unlock the room. You must enter a separate password for each Secret Room.

High Speed Internet Recommended

Because the file size for some videos, photos, and audio clips are large, for best results, you should have a broadband or high speed Internet connection. You can use dial-up, but you'll need patience.

How It Works

Step One: Go to our Web site: www.HauntedTravelsMI.com and click on "Secret Rooms." This will get you to the doorway to enter the Main Secret Room Vault. You'll see a wooden door. *CLICK ON THE DOOR HANDLE.*

Step Two: You are now in the Main Secret Room. Click on the number associated with the story, (example: The Holly Demon and Mari's Deliverance is Story #1).

Step Three: Once you click on the number, a dialogue box will come up saying you're about to enter a password protected page. *CLICK OK.*

Step Four: The Password box will come up. Carefully *ENTER THE PASSWORD* from the story, then *CLICK OK.*

Step Five: Another dialogue box will come up. If you've entered the password correctly, it will let you know. *CLICK OK.* If you've entered the wrong password, it will re-direct you back to our main page. You'll need to try again.

That's it!
You've unlocked the Story Secret Room door.
Your virtual experience begins.

Story One
The Holly Demon and Mari's Deliverance

Holly's Main Street Antiques
118 S. Saginaw St., Holly, MI
Password: mar135
Investigative Team:
Mid Michigan Paranormal Investigators

Our story of Holly's Main Street Antiques began as a standard paranormal investigation but quickly turned into something we had not anticipated. It would bring us into a world we had never seen nor want to again. The memories of what happened that night will remain with us a very long time.

A few weeks before the investigation, a gentle young mother and wife, Mari-Lynn, contacted Matt and Melanie Moyer from Mid Michigan Paranormal Investigators. She needed their help.

Mari-Lynn and Mark

Mari and her husband, Mark, own an antiques shop in Historic Holly. Her strange and unsettled visions began the minute she moved into her husband's home and began working at the antiques shop. At first it centered on the unusual disappearance of keys at the shop. From there it escalated. An antique or other object would fly off a shelf. Next came apparitions.

One of the first was in the antiques shop. It was a man dressed in a turn-of-the-century gray suit with a mustache, top hat and cane. He appeared so real that Mari thought he was a customer and asked if she could help him. As she approached, he disappeared.

Yet another was seen on the main floor. Mari described it as the image of a man without a head, hurling himself about as though on fire.

With time, different visions began appearing, becoming more frequent and erratic. The most terrifying was that of a half-lizard, half-human creature. She found it huddled in the basement of the shop. Scaled and reptilian shaped, it had human legs and arms. Seeming to be startled, it pulled human hands from its face and looked up. The eyes that met Mari's were large, wide and very human, but its face was that of a lizard. It was gone in the blink of an eye.

Her visions didn't end at the shop. She was also cursed at home. There she saw a Victorian-era woman holding a baby. Near this woman were two children, a young girl and boy between the ages of 3 and 9. They stared down from the second-floor balcony that overlooks the living room. Most disturbing is the fact these soulless apparitions had no eyes, no face. So disturbed by these spirits, Mari seldom sat in the living room. Her life had become a nightmare.

While her husband had not seen the same visions, he did admit to some strange, unexplainable happenings. Mark recalled one morning when he and Mari woke up to find several painful scratches on their bodies. The scratches could not be explained.

Mari's fears cscalated when their five-year-old son was affected. A few days previous, just before dinner, the little boy suddenly complained of a pain on his side. They lifted his shirt to see a large red mark. Very much like a burn. Mari was concerned that whatever remained in the home and business might now be going after their son.

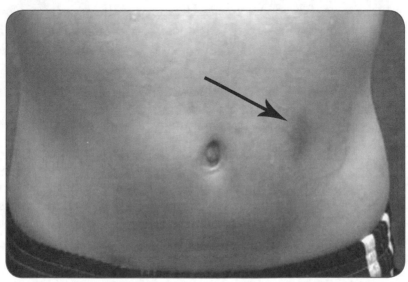

Courtesy of Mari-Lynn and Mark

Burn on Mari and Mark's son

Matt and Melanie spoke to Mari at length about her feelings and experiences. Based on that and an initial investigation of her home and business, they began to suspect there may be something to the Mari's stories. In fact, they believed it was demonic.

A demon is frequently identified as appearing human but missing certain physical characteristics. An example would be the half-human, half-lizard creature in shop's basement or the man without a head.

In their commitment to help the family, Matt and Melanie discussed the case with demonologist, G.P. Haggart. He agreed to meet with Mari and possibly perform a spiritual cleansing of the home and business.

Matt and Melanie, having worked with us on several prior occasions, thought this would be an interesting case for our book. With Mari's and Mark's approval, they invited us to join them.

This experience was something Bev and I looked at with great anticipation. We had no idea what to expect.

It was near sunset when we entered the historic village of Holly. Small, Victorian shops lined the 130-year-old street. Most of the businesses were closed for the evening and the small town was unusually quiet.

Members of Mid Michigan Paranormal Investigators were outside Holly's Main Street Antiques as our car approached. It was great to see them again. They greeted us with hugs all around and brought us in to meet Mari-Lynn and Mark.

Mark welcomed us with a warm handshake. A bit of gray hair peppered his temples and lent a distinguished, confident demeanor to his friendly smile. He then excused himself to greet the arriving minister and demonologist, G.P. Haggart.

Melanie took us to Mari, who stood quietly behind the counter of the antiques shop. The corners of her mouth quirked upward and she extended her hand on our approach. It was an honest, open smile that revealed a woman with a kind heart and gentle nature. Dark shadows brushed beneath her eyes and faint lines of tension creased her forehead belying a woman in stress.

After introductions, we asked how she was doing. Her eyes shifted downward briefly before meeting ours. "I'm doing alright, I guess." A faint blush spread across her cheeks, telling us it was far from true.

Melanie suggested we all join G.P. Haggart, who was doing the initial walk-through with Matt and Mark. We found them in the back. Matt signaled to us and made the introduction.

L to R: Mark, Mari-Lynn, Matt, J.D. Haggart discussing events

What immediately caught our attention was the pastor's unusually soft voice and deeply intense eyes that seemed to look right into your soul. He began counseling the troubled couple and asking questions about their experiences. His soothing calm provided reassurance that everything would be alright.

As Haggart continued his conversation with Mark and Mari, Matt and Melanie brought their team together to layout the plan of investigation for the evening.

The group would be split into two. One half would investigate the home and witness the cleansing while the other would investigate the store.

Watches would be synced and time carefully monitored throughout the evening. Matt and Melanie wanted to see if the cleansing or other aspects of the investigation at one location would have an effect on the other. They hoped to determine if the paranormal activity occurring at the store and home were somehow connected.

With plans finalized, the team began equipment set up. It was then Matt and Melanie took Bev and I on a tour of the shop. Holly's Main Street Antiques is a spacious store with an amazing assortment of heirlooms. From quaint figurines and unique artifacts to beautifully restored furniture dating from pre-Victorian Era to the more contemporary 1950s, 60s and 70s. There was even a small corner displaying Nazi memorabilia.

We stopped in our steps as we came across one of the more expensive items in the shop. There, encased in glass, was an early nineteenth-century vampire hunting kit. Not a toy or make-believe set, but an actual kit. There was a time in the nineteenth century when people, particularly the wealthy, became obsessed with the fear of actual vampires.

As we continued the tour, we wondered if any of the paranormal activity might be attached to some of the antiques in the shop. Matt and Melanie thought it was a possibility and hoped the investigation might provide further insight.

Our last stop was the basement. This is the area where Mari had seen the huddled, half-human creature.

We carefully made our way down worn, uneven stairs. Dampness reached from the darkness below and seemed to draw us farther downward. An aged mustiness assailed our senses as each step took us back in time.

Bev and I believe the basement is the building's soul. While the upper portions may go through many changes, the basement stands in time revealing the secrets of its past.

This basement was no different. There are two separate portions. The one in which we now stood was the oldest. Stones formed its foundation and low hanging beams required taller members of the group to keep their heads down.

Perhaps it was the disturbing appearance of this dark place that gave us a sudden sense of unease. Something wasn't right.

It was nearing 9:00 P.M. as the team got ready for the next investigation site. The moonless night did little to brighten our mood as we made our way to Mark and Mari's home.

The drive took us along a winding country road several miles from town to a contemporary home. Leaves covered the ground from a long, hard winter.

Walking up the path, we approached the entrance and noted a large, carved stone on the front porch. Its weather-bleached roughness revealed its age. Mari explained this stone was part of a cornice that had been taken from an old insane asylum. It seems Mark has an affinity for unique and sometimes bizarre artifacts. This, apparently, was one of them.

Mari invited us into their home. We entered directly into the living room. Facing us was a stairway to the second floor and, to the right, a tall, chalet-style ceiling angled upward to the second floor loft. Photographs and artwork decorated the walls. The atmosphere here was pleasant and in no way threatening.

Mari pointed to the upstairs loft. "That's were I see them." Referring, of course, to apparitions of the sightless Victorian woman and children.

Bev and I glanced upward. "Do you see them now," I asked.

She shook her head, "No. Not now."

Mari led the group through the first floor. It was comfortably homey. Accompanying us on this little tour were their five family cats. Three of them were very social and certainly did love attention! When they weren't rubbing against each other and purring, they were rubbing against us asking for scratches and strokes. We made sure they had plenty of both.

Next, Mari took us to the second level where the loft and bedrooms were located. The loft was of particular interest since this was the area where she had seen the Victorian woman and children. Right now, however, it was just a sitting room. Nothing unusual.

The last upstairs room visited was sparsely furnished. Mari explained this is where Mark's first wife stayed when she was very ill. His first wife had passed away at the hospital several years before and since then the room has remained empty.

From there, she took us to the basement. This section of the home was used as temporary storage for the antiques shop.

Collections of interesting tables, paintings and other memorabilia were stacked here and there.

Matt turned to Mari and asked, "Where's the skull?"

Making a little grimace, she pointed to a back room. "It's in there." After a slight pause, she added, "I don't like it."

Bev turned to Mari, "What kind of skull? Is it human?"

"I'm not sure, but I don't think so. My husband got it somewhere. I told him to get rid of it, but it's still here."

We followed Matt to the small room and watched as he removed a box from a top shelf. Reaching in he pulled out a partial skull and slowly turned it in his hand.

Matt and team member with the skull

Its smooth, curved shape was yellowed with age and appeared to be quite old. Based on the size and shape, it seemed fairly certain it was not the skull of a domestic animal, like a dog or cat, nor even a cow or pig. But whether or not it was human, primate or something else was anyone's guess. Mark had never had it examined by a professional. After a few minutes, Matt returned the skull to the shelf and our group returned to the main floor.

Bev and I followed Mari and Mark into the kitchen while Mid Michigan began setting up equipment. We sat and chatted for a while.

The Victorian woman and children weren't the only apparitions Mari had seen around the house. There had been others, including a man standing in the backyard by the pond.

He had worn a simple white shirt and dark pants. Mari described him as looking like a pioneer farmer. Unmoving with vacant eyes, he peered into the window.

Matt soon returned letting us know everything was ready and it was time to get started. While Bev and Matt's team headed to the antiques store, Pastor Haggart, Melanie's group and I huddled in the living room with Mari. He quietly questioned Mari all the while intently studying her every move.

As they talked, he picked up a binder and took out a piece of paper. Handing it to Mari, he asked her to read and sign it, which she did. It was a contract with God to renounce Satan. Standing, Haggart brought out a small vile of holy oil and, saying prayers, blessed the contract.

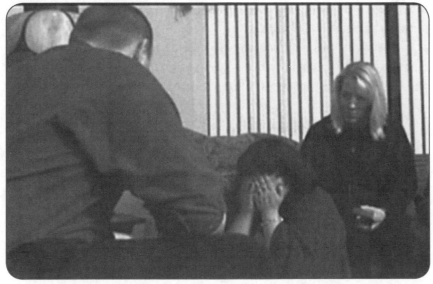

Mari breaks down after signing agreement renouncing Satan.

It was then Mari started to weep. "I can't breathe," she whispered.

He brought her to the sofa and asked her to relax. He asked why she was crying. She told him it was hard to sign the contract.

When asked what was the most difficult part, she responded, "When I had to renounce Satan. I felt so guilty."

Slowly the Pastor began drawing Mari's past into the open. What she revealed was profound and very personal. At this time, we would like to thank Mari for her bravery and willingness to let her story be told.

She grew up in a good home and loved her family. Religion was a strong part of her upbringing.

In her teenage years life became more difficult. She attended a religious school where she was subject to the relentless torment of other students. She admitted to hating the school and the associate pastor.

Angry and rebellious over her treatment, she and a couple of her friends decided to get even. They became involved in the Black Arts, using that as a means to release frustration. They signed a contract to Satan using their blood and, according to ritual, secretly buried it in the ground. When Mari and her friends went to retrieve it a few days later, it was gone. To this day Mari doesn't know what happened to it.

Though it was obvious she now felt remorse, there was still a deep-rooted hurt over what had happened. "They (the students and associate pastor) were telling me I was a sinner. So I gave my life to Satan."

The pastor brought out the Bible and said that if she would help him he would help her. Together they held the Holy Book as he had her renounce Black Magic.

Mari tearfully repeated after him, her face twisting in pain, "I renounce all the Black Magic that I have ever done to any person in Jesus' name."

Shuddering she wrapped arms around her body and bent forward, "I feel sick to my stomach."

Mari's nausea was not unexpected. According to Pastor Haggart, "When a demon exits the soul they will usually leave through the mouth; either by an uncontrollable breath, vomiting, scream, laugh or such."

Her eyes, weary, glanced upward locking onto Haggart's face, her pupils expanding into blackness, "You look weird."

"I look weird?"

"Yes, you look very weird. Like you're in a vortex."

He silently looked into her eyes then urged, "Just let it go. The pain … just let it go."

Gripping herself even harder she moaned, "It's hard to breathe."

Mari can not breathe in her distress

At this point, Haggart leaned into her, his intense eyes peering deeply into hers. Lines of concern creased his forehead. "Who's looking at me? Is this Mari?"

Placing a hand to her eyes, she weakly responded, "Yes."

"How are you feeling?"

No response. She looked up from her hands and stared at him as darkness again filled her face.

"Are you OK?" He asked.

She continued to fixate on his eyes. "I felt like I couldn't stop looking into your eyes. I can see your eyes. They're like burning through me. I want to back away."

Haggart then got up from his chair. A look of fear crossed Mari's face and she pulled farther back into the sofa. He leaned forward, eyes never leaving hers.

"You've got something in you." He whispered, gently placing the Bible on her side.

In a firm, clear voice he demanded, "Look at me."

Mari began to openly weep. "What are you doing to me!"

"Who's in there?"

Mari cried out and pulled back deeper into the sofa, "What are you doing!"

"Who's in there!" He demanded whatever was inside her to come forth.

She pulled her head away as her hand gripped her side. "It hurts."

Reverend Haggart asked, "Who's talking to me?"

In a small voice, "Me."

"Mari?"

"Yeah, it's me."

He stepped back as Mari's hands flew to her head. She gasped, "I'm sick. My head!"

Water was brought. Slowly sipping from the small cup, she looked around as if unfamiliar with her surroundings. She didn't understand why she was so upset. It wasn't as if she were afraid of God. In fact, she loved Him.

Mari explained that she felt as if she were someplace else. "What did I do?" What confused her most is the fact that she had returned to God years before and now this was happening. It didn't seem to make any sense.

Pastor Haggart explained that when you practice Black Magic you open yourself up to the devil. Once inside, it is difficult to rid yourself of its power.

He placed the Bible on her and once again began to pray. Mari lowered her head and quietly cried, a hand to the back of her neck. Once again he took the Holy oil and marked her temples.

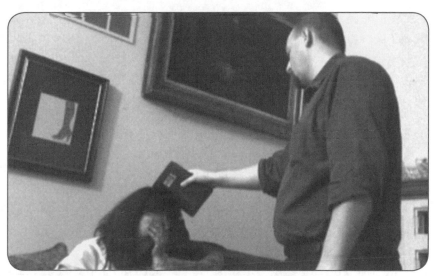

Pastor Haggart places the Bible on Mari's head.

Lifting her eyes, Mari glanced at the reverend and smiled as light returns to her face. "I can look at you now. I couldn't look at you when you were doing that."

Our group felt a small sense of relief, believing that the worst of it was over. We were wrong.

Within minutes, Mari's mood again darkened. "You look so mad at me."

Haggart told her it is Satan.

"Are you mad at me?"

"No. God loves you."

Haggart took her hands and prayed as she again began to weep then suddenly stiffened and glared at him. "Your face is black."

The pastor believed Mari was seeing him through Satan's eyes and continued to pray in an attempt to expel the demon from her body.

Suddenly the pastor's face looks black to Mari

"You have no more legal rights over this woman. I separate you now. I separate you from her!"

Again he placed the Bible on her side. Mari's reaction was fierce. Cursing vehemently she demanded to know what Haggart was doing.

"I separate you Satan from her soul. You have no legal right over her."

"This can't be happening! I'm saved."

They prayed together until Mari became sick to her stomach. To everyone's relief, a short break was taken.

When Mari finally returned to the room, her pale and expressionless face clearly reflected her current, exhausted state of mind. Ready or not, the deliverance continued.

The reverend drew the conversation back to her adolescent years. Mari began to share another unpleasant memory from her teenage years. There was a member of her family, an uncle. Everyone loved him believing him beyond reproach.

Mari, however, knew his ugly secret. She knew it from a very personal level. Molestation is a sickening word, but it is the word Mari used to describe this uncle's relationship with her. No one in the family knew or even suspected, and Mari dared not tell.

Eventually her uncle became ill. Her family went to see him. When Mari saw her uncle, she saw spirits around him. She thought they were angels. Mari feared angels and this vision was no different for her. She was frightened by their presence.

Her family believed the uncle would make a full recovery. Seeing the angels around him, Mari knew different. She was right. When he died, she confessed to being happy. "He couldn't hurt anyone anymore."

The reverend and Mari prayed that she might forgive the acts of her uncle. She clutched her chest in terrible pain. "I feel like I'm being stabbed."

He brought her to her feet and placed the Bible on her side as he demanded Satan leave. "Stop that right now! You have no more legal right. She's condemned those acts, stop holding on. Look at me. Look at me. Look at me! Let go of this one! You go when I tell you to go. Look at me."

I quickly glanced at the thermal imaging camera an investigator had focused on Mari. With some surprise, the camera revealed a white hot spot in the exact area where the Bible touched her. I looked back at Mari and the reverend.

He paused, a question in his eyes, "Who's looking at me? Is this Mari?"

No response.

"Who's looking at me?" Haggart again demanded.

My eyes shifted from the pastor to Mari. Disbelief mingled with fascination as

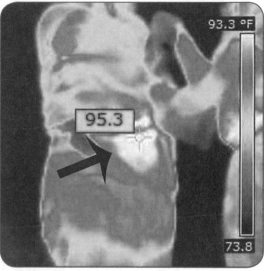

The infra red camera that measures heat shows Mari is white where the bible touches her. White is very hot.

her face changed before my eyes. Black, glazed eyes stared blankly. Her voice low, controlled said, "Piana."

Mari's face seemed to darken as she speaks the name "Piana."

Silence followed. Seconds passed and Mari's face slowly returned to normal.

He asked who Piana was.

"I don't know." Was her response.

"Do you know where you were just now?"

"Looking at you."

Her eyes again glazed over. Concerned, Haggart asked again, "Who's looking at me?"

Her simple reply, "I'm here."

"How are you feeling?"

With that question, she seemed to brighten as though a weight had been lifted. In wonder she said, "It doesn't hurt anymore."

After that, it seemed something had changed in Mari. It was a turning point. Mari no longer had negative feelings or feared Pastor Haggard. She did tell us, however, that the words "Piana, the angel" kept repeating in her mind. Chuckling lightly, she reminded us of her fear of angels.

After several additional minutes of prayer, Haggart believed they were at a point where they could stop for the evening. For some unexplainable reason, it seems Mari's utterance of the word "Piana" had removed something dark from within her. Her deliverance for this evening was over.

I was sitting on the floor with my video camera. Almost as emotionally drained as Mari. Glancing over at Melanie, the strain on her face was apparent. None of us had expected anything quite like this.

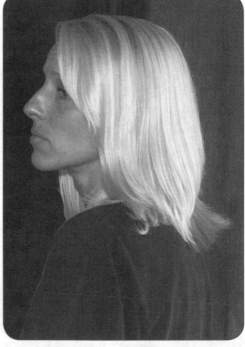

Melanie exhausted
and wondering what this all meant

Melanie decided to call Matt to see how things were progressing at the antiques store. She also wanted to let him know what had happened in the home. When she reached Matt, he told her they had a few bizarre things going on and that he would tell us all about them when we arrived.

At this point, Mari, near collapse with exhaustion, was laying back on the sofa. That's when I noticed her cats had returned to the living room. One brushed up against my leg with a loud, loving purr. It was their big cat. He urgently wanted attention.

I reached over to stroke the back of his neck and, with some surprise, noticed every hair from neck to tail was on end. I found this particularly curious but thought he might be picking up on Mari's distressed emotional state.

As the reverend began cleansing the house, our group divided to do an investigation. We ran a few EVP sessions, but nothing unusual was felt, seen or heard.

The team was packing up while Melanie and I quietly chatted in the kitchen. Mari had become ill and was in the bathroom sick to her stomach. It was at that moment we heard a low, deep moan or menacing growl from somewhere in the house. Unable to determine its origin, a search began. Eventually we came to the closed basement door. I slowly opened it to find two of her cats on the stairway.

The low growl originated from the larger cat as he towered over the smaller one two steps below. The second cat lay crouched on the lower stair. His eyes were big, obviously frightened and frozen in place. He spat out a few threatening hisses. It was a stand off.

We were shocked that these previously docile, playful cats had suddenly turned so aggressive. Not wanting to get in the mix of two angry cats, we left them alone to sort out their dominance issue.

The team was about ready to leave when a blood-curdling scream echoed up the basement stairs. The cats! We quickly returned to the basement doorway and saw the two tumbling head over heels down the stairs. They were in an intensely fierce fight, tearing and clawing at each other. Both continued the battle until their bodies slammed to the floor and then disappeared into the darkness below. Mari came over in surprise. She told us they never acted like that.

Was their anger the result of Mari's emotional turmoil, transference of her demon to them, or just two cats acting up? We could only wonder.

Unknown to us, as our group was involved with Mari's deliverance, Matt's team and Bev were investigating the antiques shop. For the most part, it had moved along smoothly though somewhat uneventful until they entered the old basement. It was shortly before 11:00 P.M. that things began to get interesting. That was just about the same time Mari's deliverance was nearing it tremulous conclusion. This section of the basement is where the half-lizard man appeared.

Matt wanted to start this portion of the investigation in the darkest, most remote section of the basement. He crawled through a whole in the stonewall that led to a small crawl space. Crouched in total darkness, he brought out his EMF and KII meters. The EVP session began.

During the first few minutes of Matt's EVP session, Bev slowly moved through the old section with a growing sense that something was about to happen. Feeling a bit uneasy, she rejoined the rest of the team as they silently watched Matt. He was summoning whatever entities or spirits might be there. That's when slight fluctuations on EMF were noticed.

Matt asked, "Are you trying to communicate with me? If you're here with me, can you come over this way, towards me?"

"Are you a demon?" Silence followed.

"Are you demonic?" Again, nothing. Though it seemed an eternity, only seconds had passed.

"I'll ask you again. Are you a demon? Are you demonic?"

The EMF jumped then, a crazy rush of flashing lights. The KII hit full red then immediately dropped. Matt felt a sudden drop in temperature, "I'm freezing," he said. They all drew near, eyes narrowed, searching the darkness. Nothing.

Matt calling out to Satan

Tension slowly ebbed. All remained quiet. Bev turned her camera towards the rear of the basement as Matt exited the crawl space.

The team moved to another area of the basement. EMF and KII meter along with audio recorders were placed on a table between them. Minutes passed, then, there it was again, another KII hit.

Knowing that KII can be affected by cell phones, Matt quickly asked everyone to check their phones. They were off. He neared the KII just as it hit again, flashing three or four lights before returning to normal.

Matt encouraged the energy to remain. "OK. So all you have to do is…" He abruptly stopped and backed away, swiping at his head and arms. "There's like something …"

Jeff, one of the investigators, seeing Matt's distressed, turned to him, "Is it attached to you, Matt?"

Suddenly frantic, he began swatting at himself, "There's something on me! There's something on me!"

"No, man," Jeff replied checking Matt over carefully.

"It's all over me!"

"There's nothing on you, dude. There's nothing on you."

Bev reinforced, "Matt, there's nothing. Matt, you're OK! Do you need to go upstairs?"

He stopped and looked at everyone while getting control of himself. "Nope."

Calming down, he apologized. "I'm sorry. Something really felt like it was all over me."

Bev asked, "Are you feeling alright now?"

"Yeah. It just felt like something ... ugh. It was like spiders hatching."

To appreciate the significance of this, it's important to understand that Matt Moyer, especially during an investigation, is a rather fearless, calm and thorough investigator. In all the time we've spent with Matt, this is the first and only time anything like this had happened.

Suddenly, looking at the MEL meter, with both EMF and temperature capabilities the group just stood and stared. This was strange. The temperature was reading 66.6. They couldn't believe what they were looking at, Satan's symbol. Normal readings for the evening were around 72 degrees.

Shortly after that the team moved up to the first floor. Batteries and video needed to be replaced. Once again the MEL meter temperature reading dropped to 66.6. Was this just a coincidence or in some mysterious way related to Mari's cleansing?

On two separate occasions the temperature lowered to 66.6 at the antiques shop, at the same time the exorcism was occurring.

The investigation continued without any measurable results. If something had been there, it was gone.

Sometime after 1:00 A.M. Melanie's team returned to the antiques shop. Bev asked, "So, how'd it go?"

Shaking my head, I said, "You have no idea. You have no idea."

Melanie firmly added, "It was absolutely horrible."

We filled Matt's team in on what happened during our time at the house. Of course, there was no way they could understand what Mari had experienced.

Many of us have seen exorcisms on television or the movies. There is, however, a huge difference between that and real life. It is incredibly draining, emotionally and physically. Both for the individual being cleansed and those witnessing the event.

Without question, Mari had difficult times in her life. It's only because of her inner-strength that she was able to turn it around and become a loving wife, mother and successful businesswoman.

But we still wondered, was it really demons that plagued Mari or her own troubled past? We have always been skeptical of deliverance/exorcism believing the problem is more mental-demons than spiritual ones. Our skepticism, at least for now, remained.

As always, history is an important part of any story we write, especially those dealing with hauntings. Sometimes we go back hundreds of years. In this case, however, we suspected history might only go back as far as Mari's past.

As a teenager, Mari had practiced Black Magic. We thought that was the only history needed. From what the reverend had suggested, Mari had opened herself to these demons. If that was true, then it seemed likely the demons would vanish after the deliverance.

Yet, it was curious that it was only after she began working in the shop and living in her husband's home that these demonic visions and strange phenomena began to occur. Perhaps some historical event connected with the home or business was feeding whatever demons lay inside of her.

Our research began. It would take us through a twisted road of lies, family secrets and one of Michigan's most sensational trials that shook the very foundation of Holly's strict Christian beliefs.

Back in 1870s, Holly was a quiet little town. The hub was centered around the hardware/general store. This was the place where locals would come to purchase daily supplies, share news and gossip.

On a late June evening, 1879, an unknown person torched the store. It wasn't the first attempt by this incendiary, but this time he was successful.

Because of the late hour no one noticed the fire until it was out of control. To make things worse, a powder magazine in the back room was consumed by the flames and exploded. The force of it blew off the roof and caused a massive fire that took out more than ten buildings and homes.

No one knew if the villain escaped or was consumed in the explosion and raging inferno that followed. Living or dead, the good people of Holly hoped that he would eventually burn in hell forever.

Through the burned rubble, the town was rebuilt including the hardware/general store. By turn-of-the-century Holly was a bustling community and the hub of village activity still remained at the hardware/general store, now owned and operated by Porter A. Wright

Though shops and small manufacturing businesses were thriving, the main occupation remained farming. The Stison's were one of the town's most prominent farming families. In fact, the Stison brothers, cousins and in-laws owned considerable farming land around Holly, Rose and White Lake.

W. Philip Stison owned and managed one of the larger farms. His brother, Charles, had his own not far away. Philip and Charles were very close and were always there to help and support each other. Philip and his wife, Nellie, did not have children and looked at Charles' two daughters, Jessie and Theresa, as part of their family.

By all accounts, Charles' youngest daughter, Theresa, was a true beauty. Shy and modest, she turned the heads of many young men in town but seemed oblivious to their glances.

In 1902, Charles and his wife, Ursula, decided to move. Theresa, didn't want to leave, at least not until she'd finished school. She asked if she could live with her Uncle Philip and Aunt Nellie. Philip and his wife were more than happy to accommodate and so Theresa came to live with them.

Theresa, now 16, was quickly turning into a lovely young woman, something that did not go unnoticed by her Uncle Philip. Teasing and light flirtations moved the two in a direction that was forbidden.

Philip's wife was the first to notice the unnecessary and unseemly attention Philip was pouring on Theresa. Though he denied it, Nellie knew the signs. She vehemently voiced her disgust at their sinful actions and couldn't understand what possessed him.

It is likely she blamed Theresa for her husband's deviance. In turn-of-the-century America, it was believed the woman was the seducer or temptress and the man the victim.

In any event, Philip's wife left him and Theresa remained at the home. Almost two years had passed until, one day, Theresa simply vanished. When her family and friends asked Philip what had become of her, he told them he didn't know. At least, that was what Philip said.

The mystery of Theresa's disappearance continued for several months. It ended in March of 1904 when Porter A. Wright, owner of Holly's hardware/general store, received a letter from the Reed City Sanitarium. The communication informed him that a young girl died at their institution. In her possession was an unsigned letter written on letterhead from Mr. Wright's store. They asked him if he had further information on the girl.

We're not certain what Wright told them, but it seems apparent that he knew something of what was going on between Theresa and Philip. The two had been sending anonymous letters to each other and Wright seemed to be the go between for their clandestine communications.

What would be learned is that Theresa Stison was staying at the institution under an assumed name. She had died several days after childbirth. The suspected father of her child was, of course, Philip.

A complaint was immediately filed against Philip Stison on charges of incest. Knowing of his impending arrest, Philip fled. The town of Holly, incensed over what had happened, set up a reward for his capture.

Authorities tracked him to a small island in Canada where he was found hiding in a cabin. Definitely not eager to give up, he had a shotgun and was ready to fight. They eventually overcame his resistance without injury. According to newspaper reports, upon his arrest Stison indicated he hadn't slept a night since he left Holly.

The trial that followed was quite sensational and reported in newspapers throughout the Midwest. People of Holly were enraged over Stison's unforgiveable actions.

The courtroom was full throughout the duration of the trial. During testimony it was brought out that Theresa, on her deathbed, admitted Philip Stison was the father of her child. Adding to the damning evidence was testimony from a young boy, approximately nine years old, who had been living with the Stisons at the time. Within 90 minutes of the trial's conclusion, the jury reached a verdict. Guilty as charged.

Stison's attorney immediately filed an appeal on inadmissible hearsay evidence. They claimed the dying words of Theresa, coming from a secondary source, should not have been allowed.

Michigan's Supreme Court eventually overturned the verdict indicating a retrial was needed that would exclude Theresa Stison's dying admission. A re-trial never occurred. Waterman Philip Stison was free, never paying for his crime, and never again returning to Holly.

Whether or not Theresa's relationship with her uncle was one of mutual consent or a situation in which she felt trapped will never be known. Also unknown is the fate of her baby. Did the innocent child die shortly after birth or end up in an orphanage?

When we began our research, we never expected to find such a startling sequence of events or learn the uncanny connection between Theresa Stison and Mari. Let's put the pieces together.

As Mari had told us, her visions began from the moment she moved into Mark's home and started working at the antiques shop. What we discovered is that Mark and Mari's home was built on what was once Philip Stison's farm.

The emotional link between Theresa and Mari is somewhat obvious. Both were quiet, modest women plagued with internal feelings of guilt and sin, shamed by what their uncle had done.

If the Victorian era woman Mari sees is real, then Theresa's spirit could be reaching out to her through this powerful, emotional connection. The infant in her arms many believed was conceived and born in sin.

Then there's the eight or nine year old boy with the woman and infant. This reminds us of the young boy who lived at the Stison home. Over the nearly two-years Theresa lived with Philip, the boy and she formed a close bond. It was this boy who testified against Philip in court and helped the jury decide on the guilty verdict. Interestingly, we were not able to find further record of the boy after the trial. Could the spirits of Theresa, her baby and the young boy be unable to rest, waiting for justice?

Unknown is the apparition of a little girl with the Victorian woman that Mari has seen with the baby and young boy. There were several children who died in the Stison family, including one little girl nearly three years old. Whether or not she's the one in Mari's vision remains a question.

We also discovered an uncanny connection between the Stison saga and Mark and Mari's antiques shop. It seems that Holly's Main Street Antiques shop is the former Porter A. Wright hardware/general store. P.A. Wright was the middleman in Philip Stison's plot to cover up Theresa's pregnancy. How bizarre that Mari would find her way into that shop and that home. It's as if fate has pulled her in this direction.

At first we considered the possibility that Mari's demons at the shop were attached to an antique. Now we're not sure. There could be another possibility.

If there are spirit entities remaining at the shop, is there something in Mari drawing them out? Mari's Black Magic practices and current fragile state may have unknowingly opened a door to the past that released dark memories. The apparition of the man moving frantically as though on fire could be the spirit of the arsonist who started the Holly fire of 1879.

If the half-human creature does exist in the shop's basement, it may be another manifestation brought from some other time. Who knows how long this inhuman being has lurked within the aged stone walls of this place.

Evidence review began. We hoped to discover if the visions Mari had seen would be validated with evidence collected during the investigation. Whatever doubts Bev and I had about demons, possessions, exorcism and deliverance would soon begin to crumble.

"Piana." That was the single, eerie word hissing through the audio recorded in the basement of the antiques shop. To our astonishment, this EVP was the exact name Mari called out during the culmination of her deliverance several miles away. Perhaps even more surprising, the EVP occurred within minutes of her utterance.

What would shake us even more was the word captured just twenty seconds later. From the blackness of the basement's crawl space, we heard Matt's voice, "Are you a demon?"

The response, "Satan."

EMF levels began to fluctuate. Matt asked if a presence was trying to communicate with him. It seems that it had.

We listened intently as Matt continued to call off EMF changes and then levels went flat. As Matt tells us, the previous night he had a dream in which the name Leonard came up. He felt it might be related to this case, so he asked, "Is your name Leonard?"

The whispered response, again the word "Satan."

With that, Matt called off an EMF spike and voiced his surprise when the KII's lights shot up to red. The air around Matt became suddenly chilled. No one heard and no one suspected that something evil might be near.

Not fully understanding the significance of the EMF spikes in the basement, the group eventually made their way upstairs. It was then the next piece of audio evidence was captured. Over the sound of shuffling feet and general chatter we heard a foreign, gruff voice, "Let's see."

The words were clear but didn't seem to respond to the conversation of Matt's group. Had they interrupted a ghostly conversation?

Additional EVPs were collected during the investigation. All evidence along with video clips and photographs, including those taken during Mari's deliverance, can be seen and heard in our Web site's Secret Room.

As Bev and I finish this story, we contemplate Mari's deliverance.

During that long, exhausting evening, Mari forgave the transgressions of those who hurt her, including her uncle. Since then, a darkness has been lifted from her. Though there are still unusual phenomena happening around the shop and home, she is no longer afraid.

Perhaps most interesting, since the deliverance, Mari hasn't seen the Victorian woman and children in her home. They seem to have vanished. Perhaps Mari's deliverance was Theresa's as well.

Story Two
The Italian Hall Disaster and Calumet Theater

240 6th Street, Calumet, MI
Password: ihd1319

We left in the early morning hours to investigate the Calumet Theater in Michigan's Upper Peninsula. Kat and I would be going solo on this hunt and not joining another team. Certainly this was not the first investigation we would do on our own but was one of the more complex. There would be a lot of ground to cover for two people.

Lost in our thoughts, we were unusually quiet during the long road trip. Our somber mood wasn't from the theater's supposed cadre of spirited entertainers but rather the Italian Hall Disaster of December 24, 1913. Let's go back in time to Calumet's early days.

Calumet, then the village of Red Jacket, was a growing and prosperous community at the turn of the century with the world's largest copper producing mine. Mine owners and the village were getting wealthier with each day. It got to a point where the municipal leaders felt the town deserved its own opera house. After all, what well-to-do city didn't have one? In 1897 the Red Jacket Opera House was built over the municipal offices in the center of town. It quickly became the hub of activity.

With the city's increasing wealth, town officials began to wonder if the opera house was grand enough. Work soon began on an expansion. When completed in 1900, the Calumet Opera House was one of Michigan's most elegant theaters. It boasted many modern amenities such as heat, electrical lights and an impressive seating capacity of 1200.

While city leaders and mine owners enjoyed this beautiful theater and many other luxuries, the miners were struggling underground. There was a growing discontent over wages and working conditions.

These hard-working men earned half of what other miners were making across the country. The owners grew richer while the miners worked long hours in terrible conditions. Injury and death became an accepted part of the job.

The miners' discontent opened the door, in 1908, for the West Federation of Miners (WFM) to come in and unionize the workers. This was the beginning of a growing dispute and anger between union workers, non-union workers, management and business leaders. Those opposed to the union were called The Alliance.

MTU Archives and Copper Country Historical Collection, Michigan Technological University

The original Calumet Theater/Red Jacket Opera House

In the summer of 1913, union and management couldn't agree on wage and labor issues. The union called a strike that idled over 15,000 workers. Miners thought the strike would end quickly, but they were wrong. Owners brought in non-union workers and by early December there still was no resolution in sight. Violence erupted that many believed was incited by The Citizens Alliance. Michigan's Governor Ferris, concerned over the growing danger, decided to send in more than 2,600 National Guards to try and calm the city.

With constant fighting and lack of income, conditions were deteriorating for union workers and their families. Families were going without the bare necessities that included food and heat. With Christmas fast approaching, parents were afraid they wouldn't be able to afford gifts and traditional festivities for their children.

Because of the dire situation, the Women's Auxiliary decided to throw a Christmas party for the town's children. Annie Clemec, known as Big Annie, was the Auxiliary president and coordinator of the event.

It was decided the party would be held at The Italian Hall, which served as the headquarters for Calumet's Benevolent Society. At that time, Calumet was a melting pot of immigrants such as Finish, Polish, Italian, Croatian, Swedish and many others. The Society encouraged and provided financial aid to Calumet's immigrant population. It also gave relief to victims of hardship. Many of the miners were new to the country, didn't speak English, and needed help to adjust. So naturally, the Italian Hall would be the perfect site for the event.

It was early afternoon on Christmas Eve, 1913 when the crowd started to form. More than 600 people, mostly children, jammed in a room that should have held half that number. The hall was so full, people were crushed together. Some children fainted for lack of air. No one anticipated this kind of crowd.

The program that day was to include a play, caroling, candy and Christmas trees. The highlight would be when Santa came and gave all the children a gift.

As the afternoon progressed, the youngsters, in their eagerness, began to push towards the stage. Big Annie tried to control the children; but they were just too excited. It was decided to shorten the program. After leading a few carols, Santa arrived and began distributing gifts. That's when the children excitedly rushed the stage. Annie called out that if they didn't get back no one would get anything.

It was during this chaos that a man came up from the stairs and entered the room. No one paid attention until he yelled, "Fire … fire!" One of the parents, Mrs. Shiver, knowing there was no fire tried to quiet him down. He turned from her and was gone.

Mayhem instantly broke out. The cry of fire exploded across the hall. Pushing through the panic-driven crowds, frantic parents rushed to find their children. Others charged the single staircase in a desperate effort to get out.

MTU Archives and Copper Country Historical
Collection, Michigan Technological University

Over 600 children and their families crowded this small area.
The photo was taken the day after.

Big Annie tried to reassure the crowd without success. Mrs. Shiver began to play the piano hoping the music would calm the people, but their fear was uncontrollable. Cries and screams were heard as scores tumbled down the stairs and were crushed by those tripping over them

The shrieks and wails of the living were mingled with the screams of the dying. The whole mass turned and lifted in a struggle to exit the stairway. Bodies piled upon bodies extending 30 feet up the staircase and nearly reaching the ceiling. Those that remained alive couldn't move and were barely able to breathe. Most suffocated while others were crushed to death. In their crazed state, few thought of using the fire escape to reach safety.

Within minutes, Second Assistant Chief, Jacob Kaiser, arrived on the scene. This is where the eyewitness accounts become confusing. Some reports indicated rescuers couldn't open the front door to assist the people because bodies blocked the door.

Yet other witness accounts indicated that rescuers opened the doors but couldn't remove the bodies because of the horrific tangle of human limbs. Looking at the huge mass on the stairs it was hard to tell where one body ended and another began.

The stairs where 74 people, mostly children, lost their lives.
Bodies were stacked to the ceiling.

Regardless of the reason, Kaiser and others rushed up the fire escape to the second floor. They were met with sheer chaos and had to claw their way to the staircase. Men, women and children ran about the room screaming while others continued to rush down the stairs to their death. In an attempt to gain control and calm the panic, in a loud booming voice Kaiser called for the people to settle down. There was no danger. The rescue party began untangling the living, injured and dead. It seemed to take an eternity.

The deceased were laid out in front of the Italian Hall where an already huge, frenzied crowd was waiting to see what had happened to their children. Emotion gripped those searching for their loved ones. Some parents, in their haste and grief, rushed their lifeless little one home only to later realize the child was not theirs.

It was obvious to the rescue team that leaving the dead outside was making things much worse. The decision was made to use the Red Jacket Opera House as a temporary morgue. The hall, normally filled with music and laughter, was soon filled with the bodies of innocent children, women and men and the tears of hopeless people. In the end, 74 lost their lives, 56 were children.

Sometime during that dreadful night, a photographer took a picture of the youngest victims laid on the stage. When the film was developed, the photographer noticed an unusual glow surrounding the bodies of the children. The picture was simply titled "Angels". This photograph gained national recognition. After that, the people of Calumet and across the nation used the word "angels" when they spoke of the innocent children lost on that terrible Christmas Eve.

It was a dark and bleak Christmas in Calumet.

A mass funeral was arranged for the majority of the dead. It would take several days to prepare. The Western Federation of Miners covered the cost of burial, but it took time to raise the funds. More importantly, there were not enough caskets in the area and families had to wait for coffins to be brought in from other towns. The funeral was December 29, 1913.

All of Calumet was in mourning that day. Bells tolled as funeral services were held throughout the city. Tens of thousands came to mourn. The supply of hearses and vehicles was inadequate, so scores of union members carried the white coffins holding children.

Cold winds cut through the long procession of mourners as they slowly made their way across the frozen ground to the snow-shrouded cemetery not far from Lake Superior. The funeral procession extended for blocks.

Once the dead were laid to rest the search for the guilty began. Inquest testimony was clouded. A few people thought the

The Italian Hall in Mourning, the Next Day After Disaster

On Christmas Day people stood in the snow mourning the town's loss.

man who yelled fire was wearing an Alliance button and others disagreed. Adding to that, no one recognized the man. There were also conflicting statements about what he looked like and wore.

Blame was thrown back and forth. To this day the man remains unidentified and the reason for his actions a mystery. Eventually the strike was resolved, but the town would never be the same, nor would the union.

Funeral Parade of the Victims Heading to the Cemetery

Thousands followed the funeral procession.

Over the decades, as copper mining in Calumet declined so did the city's wealth and population. Today Calumet's population hovers around 1,000 residents, far less than its 25,000 during the city's copper mining heyday.

It was late afternoon as Kat and I entered this historic town, our thoughts swinging back to the present. I slowly drove the car passed vacant lots and quiet streets. Calumet was almost a ghost town compared to its bustling days as the copper mining capital of the world. Glimpses of its former glory could still be seen in some of its remaining architecture.

Driving through the town what we failed to notice, in passing, was a small lot with a lonely, sandstone arch. Its significance was completely lost to us. We would later learn that this marked the location of the Italian Hall and was the sole reminder of that fateful Christmas Eve nearly one hundred years ago.

Traffic increased as we neared the Calumet Theater. With copper prominently displayed in its roof and cornices, this two-story renaissance revival structure clearly stood out from many of the other buildings in town. It immediately caught our eye as we turned onto 6th Street.

Laura Miller, Executive Director, greeted us at the theater's main entrance. We asked her if traffic was always this busy around the theater and she chuckled, "The Theater always has something going on."

Entering the main auditorium, we paused as our eyes scanned the amazing interior of this magnificent, historic theater. In our travels, we have been to many grand theaters and opera houses. The Calumet Theater ranks among the most impressive. Hand painted murals and gold inlays sweep up to curved, vaulted ceilings. Rows of seats lined the expansive room and upper balconies. Private booths peak from corners near the stage, each holding two white wicker chairs.

Its historic elegance has been meticulously restored by the non-profit Calumet Theater Company. This company leases the theater from the city. It is the only theater in the country that was and still is municipally owned. Financial support from the community and grants are used to maintain this historic theater.

The opulent stage indicates the former wealth of Calumet.

Moving into the auditorium actors were rehearsing on stage for the upcoming play, Death of a Salesman. With a finger to her lips, so as not to disturb the actors, she ushered us into her office. Waiting inside was her friend Art. They would be our guides for the evening.

As we talked Laura explained she has been with the Calumet Theater for some time. She loves its history and beauty along with the creative energy of the performances. She is heavily involved with the Friends of Calumet Theater fundraising group dedicated to preserving its beauty and history.

Laura began telling us about the theater and some of its ghostly stories. Over the years there have been many tales from patrons, workers and volunteers.

The first encounter with the paranormal involved the theater's marketing director. It happened one afternoon just after a group of students from the high school left the theater. The art director was on stage and glanced towards the balcony. He saw a figure go by. Thinking it was one of the students, he went up to the balcony but no one was there. This happened to him once more when he was with another person. This time they both saw the figure.

The apparition of a man has been seen in the basement and people have felt cold spots. No one knows who the man is or why he remains.

People also hear music in the theater. The apparition of a woman in a beautiful formal gown is frequently

Laura Miller, Executive Director responsible for much of the work and fundraising necessary to maintain the theater.

seen and heard. We asked Laura who she thought the woman was. Without hesitation she responded, "Madame Modjeska."

Helena Opid was born in Krakow, Poland in 1840. She would eventually marry her guardian, actor Gustave Sianmier, and took his stage name, Modrzejewska, eventually shortened to Modjeska.

Helena was a world-renowned Shakespearean actress who spent much of her later years performing in the United Sates and resided in California. She came to the Calumet Theater on three separate occasions.

Laura explained, "She was very fond of the Calumet Theater." In surprise I mention, "But she was only here three times."

Laura explained why Madame Modjeska was here. She always wanted to play the female lead, Kate, in Taming of the Shrew but never had the opportunity. In the 1950s Taming of the Shrew was being performed at the theater. Actress Adysse Lane was the lead female and unfortunately forgot her lines in one scene. Laura said, "Her spirit (Madame Modjeska) was there, and when Adysse lost her lines Madame supposedly mouthed the words (to Adysse)."

Since then many people claim to have seen and heard Madame. It is said she becomes particularly annoyed when her beautifully framed picture is moved. This picture is on the back wall of the auditorium and a favorite of photographers. Laura mentioned that very frequently the photographer's camera freezes, the battery is drained or the picture doesn't come out.

When speaking of the paranormal activity at the Calumet Theater, she talked about Kathy Lynch. Kathy is the founder of G.H.O.S.T. Paranormal Society in the Upper Peninsula. Her team has investigated the theater on several occasions. Laura mentioned that her and Kathy along with other team members had experiences during investigations. The result of those investigations were a number of EVPs. We were looking forward to hearing them at a later time.

What peaked our attention was listening to Laura recount the paranormal activity in the ballroom. This section of the theater was the original Red Jacket Opera House. Many of the EVPs from G.H.O.S.T. were actually collected here.

Laura told the story of one particular investigation with G.H.O.S.T. in the ballroom. Five of them sat at a table leaving one empty chair. Kathy began talking to the spirits, "Is there any one here? Could you give us a sign? Please sit down and join us."

Suddenly the two investigators sitting on either side of the vacant chair felt a sudden chill emanating from the empty seat. Laura said the temperature dropped about 30 degrees and stayed that way for a few minutes. According to Laura, after reviewing audio, Kathy captured several distinct EVPs.

Madam Modjeska is said to haunt the theater.

Kat and I were eager to start the investigation. After concluding the tour with Laura and Art, we laid out our plans. With just two IR video cameras and three digital audio recorders, positioning was critical. Since most of the activity occurred in the auditorium and ballroom, those would be our areas of focus. One camera would stay with us. The second was positioned on the stage viewing the auditorium and balconies, where reported apparitions have been seen.

One audio recorder was placed on the second balcony, another in the auditorium and the third in the ballroom. An IR video camera stationed on the stage would serve as a fourth audio device and capture any movement in the auditorium's main floor and balconies. A second IR video camera, two digital still cameras, an EMF meter and thermo gage would stay with us.

Over the decades there have been many reports of paranormal activity. We now wondered, with anticipation, if we could confirm stories of the Calumet Theater's haunting. The investigation began.

Laura asked if we wanted the lights turned off. For many paranormal teams, that is the only way they investigate. Kat and I believe there are benefits to that. We also believe there are benefits to investigating by recreating the conditions in which paranormal activity is experienced. Since apparitions were seen in the main auditorium with the lights partly on, that's the condition we wanted for the auditorium. During the night regular EMF and temperature readings would be taken to establish base readings and help identify unusual spikes that might indicate activity during the evening.

Gathering in the auditorium, Kat took a position on stage bringing an EMF meter. I sat in the first row with a thermo gage. Laura and Art were in the back.

Kat started by calling out Madam's name, asking if she would respond with a knock. Several minutes pasted in silence. Then Kat asked if the spirit of someone from the Calumet Theater was with us. She called for any performers to come forward. There was no noticeable response.

An attempt to recreate an event or talk about something familiar to the spirit's past is frequently used to draw them out. This would be our next approach.

I asked Laura to talk about the early days of the theater and she told us about the first performance in March 1900. It was the comedy, The Highway Men. As Laura began talking about Madam Modjeska and her fame as an actress, Kat noticed EMF levels began to rise. She encouraged Laura to continue.

It was at that point Kat asked Art if he thought Madam Modjeska was beautiful. Art said, "No, not really." Kat glanced at the EMF and laughed, "I don't know if she's with us... but the EMF went down to zero." At the same time Kat felt coolness and noticed a sudden temperature drop from 62 to 57 degrees. Was it paranormal of just the chill of the night setting in?

Kat asked if some of the famous people who had performed in the theater were there, such as Sara Barnhart and Lon Chaney. Again, no response.

We thought the performers might need a little encouragement to come out. Everyone gave them a big round of applause, but if there were spirits around they continued to be elusive.

The investigation would now move to the upper balconies. We settled on the second floor balcony, where the marketing director had seen a shadow on two separate occasions.

This shadowy vision may have simply been a trick of the eye, but maybe not. The Red Jacket Ballroom, which served as a temporary morgue after the panic, can be entered from this level. We wondered, if there really was a shadow, could it be a lost soul from 1913?

Kat put the EMF meter on the floor as we began asking questions. Approximately 30 minutes into our session we began noticing slight EMF fluctuations. At first, neither Kat nor I paid much attention until we realized these minor changes correlated directly to questions about children.

Kat asked if the spirit was that of an adult male or female. EMF remained flat. When asked if it was a little girl, EMF remained flat. EMF began to move when Kat's questions centered around a little boy.

"Were you a little boy between the ages of six and eight?" The EMF ticked upward. We looked at each other with growing anticipation. Was it a response?

"Were you younger than six? Were you five?"

The EMF dropped to zero.

Kat resumed her upward age count, but the EMF remained flat.

"Were you at the Italian Hall December 24th?" In silence we watched as the EMF levels once again elevated.

Laura asked, "Were you here to watch movies? There were lots of movies." EMF immediately dropped to zero.

Levels remained flat through a series of questions. It seemed If anything had been with us, it was now gone. We decided to move to the next location.

Just after 1:00 a.m. we entered the ballroom. Moonlight cast a ghostly pallor across the stage that once held the bodies of victims from that Christmas Eve so long ago. There was a certain chill that went beyond the coolness of the room. None of us today could possibly understand the horror and pain that occurred in this place now so quite and still.

Laura pointed to a table in the center of the room. This is where Kathy and her team had collected evidence on a prior investigation. We chose the same location in an attempt to recreate a similar environment. An audio recorder was placed on the table.

There is no denying that we felt a change, heaviness in the atmosphere. In the dark Kat began to set up her video recorder. I told the spirits to wait, "Don't show yourself until the camera's ready."

Kat responded, "Oh, that they should be so kind." A whispered response remained unheard.

Our EVP session began in earnest when Laura invited the spirits to join us. Silence followed.

Then I said, "Who are you?" Again silence.

We sat quietly. Seconds drifted into minutes as time passed.

Eventually, Laura pointed to an upper balcony where band or orchestra members used to play. She explained that strange lights had been seen in that area. Noting windows faced the street, we thought perhaps it might be passing reflections from car lights. Not long after, a car did pass by and its lights did reflect on the wall. This identified a possible reason.

We resumed to our silent vigil until Kat's next question, "Were you part of the Italian Hall Panic? Did you lose someone? Did you die?"

For a moment nothing, and then a faint sound, a whisper. It was none of us. Just our imagination? Only later would we know.

EMF and temperature were checked. Kat was about to tell us the EMF had spiked but halted in mid sentence. "I think I just saw a shadow back there. Right against the window," she whispered. Immediately vigilant, our eyes turned toward the window. Nothing. Laura commented this had been a very active area on the last investigation.

Stage, Red Jacket Opera House.
Location where many bodies were placed after the Italian Hall Disaster.

Taking the EMF meter from the table, Kat moved to the stage. Everything was normal. The video camera was pointed in that direction. If there had been a shadow, it would be captured.

There was a sense among us that something was waiting to happen. It was about 1:45 A.M. Activity seemed to be rising. I heard something. A whisper. I asked if anyone else heard it. They hadn't.

This is the challenging part of investigations. There is always some point when your eyes and ears begin playing tricks. Is that what was happening to us? Sometimes it is only in evidence review when you find the truth.

If there was spirit activity here, we hoped to stir it up by recounting the tragic events of December 24, 1913. At that point in our conversation, Kat called out, "Is the person who yelled fire at the Italian Hall Disaster with us tonight? Are you a coward?"

Time continued to slip away. Shortly after 2:30 A.M., we decided to call it a wrap. Laura, Art, Kat and I were exhausted. Thanking them for their help, we packed our equipment and headed off for some much needed rest. All of us hoped something had been recorded that evening.

The outside air was cool and damp. Streetlights cast a sickly yellow pallor over the empty streets. It is a time of night when some say only the dead are alive. How true those words seemed to us now.

Earlier in the evening Laura told us where the Italian Hall memorial was located. Driving down the road, we turned the corner and stopped at the memorial site. It seemed the whole city was asleep but us. Moonlight reflected off the archway and lonely bronze marker on this tiny plot of land. Impossible. Impossible to imagine this small lot was the site of the Italian Hall and Calumet's most horrible disaster.

The chill cut right through us was we walked under the arch and entered hallowed grounds. Our time here lasted only 10 minutes. Exhausted, the motel seemed an eternity away.

Over breakfast the next morning, we discovered the Italian Hall audio file was blank. The decision was made to return to the site. Unintentionally, we arrived about the same time the families arrived that fateful Christmas Eve in 1913. This time Kat and I came prepared with two audio recorders, camera and video recorder. The cluster of small homes lining the streets near the memorial site were quiet.

A few questions were asked, but mostly we just sat and listened. The only sound heard was the wind swirling around the leafless tree. Thirty minutes later, we gathered our equipment and left. We never looked back.

Driving up to Calumet had been a quiet and pensive time for us. That was not the case going back. We chatted nearly non-stop and somehow made the eleven-hour drive in about nine.

We expected to begin reviewing recorded materials shortly after returning. Unfortunately, our business kicked into high gear. As weeks passed, Kat and I seemed to forget about the events that transpired the night of our Calumet investigation. It quickly came back as we began reviewing video, audio and photographs. The evidence collected that evening and following day could not have been anticipated.

The original Italian Hall arch
and this small memorial are the only reminders of that fateful day .

Let's return to the night's chain of events. The investigation began on the first floor. Kat was on the stage and I was in the first row. Laura and Art sat in back. We started talking about Madam Modjeska. Kat noticed the EMF levels began to elevate and she felt a cold spot. Kat asked Art if he thought Madam was beautiful. He casually replied, "No not really." Moments later our audio picked up a voice. We believe in may say "Modjeska." It's a little odd because it appears to be Madam's name but ending in an "o" (Modjesko). Could the stories of Madam's spirit remaining be true?

Our time in the balcony also had its surprises.

Headphones in place, Kat and I were listening to audio in our respective offices when I felt a tap on my shoulder. I looked up to see her pointing to her office and followed as she disappeared around the corner.

She sat quietly sitting at the computer holding out headphones as I entered. "We got a response," was all she said.

I positioned the earphones, as Kat began the audio clip. We were on the second balcony. EMF levels were fluctuating. I heard Kat's voice ask if the spirit was a boy between the age of 6 and 8. The audio hissed white noise for a moment, then a long, drawn out response, "Yes." Shortly after, I can hear Kat's voice saying EMF levels had risen.

I glanced at Kat. She nodded, "There's more."

The next audio clip was played. The sound of Kat's voice was heard asking if the boy was 10, 11 or 12. The hushed voice again responded. This time the word I heard was, "No."

Yet another clip was played. "Were you at the Italian Hall Panic?" Kat asked. Several second passed with only the empty sound of white noise. I looked up thinking I had missed the EVP. I saw Kat mouth the word, "Wait." It was then I heard it, the long, drawn out response, "Yeees." Followed by Kat's voice saying EMF levels had risen.

It seemed there was someone on the balcony with us that night. But who it was remains a mystery. It was particularly strange that the voice sounded more like an adult male than a young boy. If we ever return for another investigation, we will certainly expand our questioning to hopefully learn more.

Verbal responses weren't the only things captured on audio. Additional sounds were recorded after we left the balcony. One thing heard was unusual music, much like what you would expect to hear at a silent movie, or from a gramophone. This lasted for several minutes. It had a tinny, disjointed sound. We don't know its cause and after Laura reviewed the sound she had no idea where it came from but Laura did tell us the marketing director often heard music in the auditorium. Perhaps this is what he hears.

While Kat continued to review her audio, I loaded the segment from the ballroom into my computer. After getting so many unexpected EVPs in the theater, I was anxious to review the audio from the ballroom, the original Red Jacket Opera House. If spirits or their energy remain anywhere within these walls, it seems they would be in the ballroom. After all, this room was the culmination of the towns biggest tragedy.

I would not be disappointed. The first recording came at 12:05 A.M., just minutes after we left the recorder in the room. It was a single, mournful word, "Angel." As the hushed voice came through the headphone, I had to fight back a sudden sense of remorse. Through research and reading eyewitness accounts, we had learned the dead children were often referred to as Angels.

At 12:23 A.M. another disembodied voice was captured. Again it was a single word, "Annie." Was the voice calling out to Big Annie, Anna Clemec the Auxiliary President who had arranged the Christmas Eve party? Big Annie desperately attempted to calm everyone during the panic. Could someone be calling out to her even now?

Another EVP was captured shortly after 1:00 A.M. The four of us had entered the ballroom and Kat began to set up her camera. At that point I remarked, "We'd love to talk to you. Don't show yourself until the camera's up." The very obliging response was, "Happy to."

Time slipped away as I eagerly continued the ballroom audio. I heard Kat ask if there was anyone with us from the panic and if they died. A few seconds later, the soft hiss of "yes" was recorded.

Unfortunately the shadow Kat thought she'd seen against the ballroom window was not seen on video. It was dismissed as a common problem with ghost hunting, seeing things in the dark that simply aren't there. We believed that until, just moments after Kat thought she saw a shadow, a voice was heard, "Hope they get it." The voice sounded as if it spoke directly into the recorder. Is it possible that at least one spirit is hoping the shadow was captured on video? To this day we wonder why.

Having finished her audio review, Kat came into my office and sat down. "So, what are you finding?"

"More than we would have expected," was my response.

After listening to the evidence I had turned up, we sat down together to finish the ballroom audio.

Other EVPs were captured in the ballroom including the voice of a child, a woman and a voice speaking over our conversation. There are different interpretations of what they're saying. These EVPs can be heard in our Secret Room.

It was near the end of our time in the ballroom, the last few minutes of time code clicked away. It's then one of the strongest EVPs was captured. Kat asked if the person who yelled fire at the Italian Hall was a coward.

We heard nothing that night sitting in the dark. It seems we were wrong. But then we've come to learn so much in the paranormal eludes our natural and limited senses. On audio the response was clear as was its message. A lifeless, male voice repeated, "Coward."

As the last moments of audio faded, we sat there stunned at the amount of evidence captured. Kat and I have been on over 100 investigations since we began writing about our ghost hunting experiences. We both agree this ranks as one of our top paranormal locations. It is very possible that the Calumet Theater has both residual and intelligent spirits residing within its walls.

The evidence doesn't end here. Perhaps the most profoundly touching EVPs were collected during our brief time at the Italian Hall Memorial Site. There were just three little words, but they were profoundly touching, "Momma" and "Johnny … Johnny?" Several children named Johnny died on December 24, 1913. Was this one of them? We pause, as this story ends and wonder, did they ever find each other?

Story Three
The Crouch Murders

Reynolds Cemetery, Jackson, MI
St. Johns Cemetery, Jackson, MI
Crouch Homestead
(address withheld by owner request)
Password: cm324
Historical Assistance: Jeff Westover

November 21, 1883, it was near 11:00 P.M. Rolling storm clouds obliterated what little light the evening sky offered and cast the land in an inky blackness. Growling winds rushed across empty fields and sent a flurry of fallen leaves scratching against the farmhouse windows as though begging entry. Inside two men sat socializing, glasses of cider in hand, seemingly unaware of the impending storm.

The old man was Jacob Crouch, family patriarch and one of Jackson County's most prominent citizens. The younger was Moses Polley, a former employee of Jacob Crouch. Since leaving Jacob's employment, young Polley had married, moved to Pennsylvania and achieved success in the cattle buying business. Jacob had done business with Moses in the past and, after selling some fine stock, invited Polley to spend the night.

Jacob's youngest and favorite daughter, Eunice, and her husband, William Henry White, had retired earlier. Eunice, in her ninth month of pregnancy, needed as much rest as possible. The Crouch housekeeper, Julia Reese, was also asleep in her room off the kitchen as was, George Bolles, the seventeen-year-old African American hired hand who slept upstairs.

Sometime after 11:00 P.M. the two men turned in for the night. Jacob gave his bed to Moses and went to sleep in an alcove near the front of the house. Though the winds howled and the sound of distant thunder rumbled, the Crouch household slept peacefully.

A flash of lighting momentarily brightened the obsidian sky casting an eerie light across the fields. If anyone had looked out at that moment they might have seen dark shadows moving deeper into the barn. Eyes watched as the storm began its violent path.

The next morning, November 22, 1883, Ray Clements looked out his window into the cold, gray morning to survey the damage from the previous night's storm. Surprised, his eyes locked on George Bolles running frantically down the street. The young black man wore no shoes, coat or hat. Ray called out to him and, seeing Ray, he turned and came over. Breathlessly he asked if Ray had seen Whitey (referring to Henry White, Eunice's husband). Ray said no. It was then George told him someone had broken into the house the previous night, and he thought everyone had been murdered.

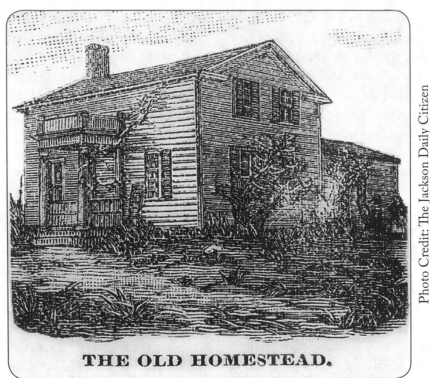

THE OLD HOMESTEAD.

Photo Credit: The Jackson Daily Citizen
Courtesy of Gerry Blanchard

A rendering of Jacob Crouches 1800's home.

George quickly shared his story. He had gone to bed at a little after 8:00 P.M. Sometime between 1:00 A.M. and 3:00 A.M. he was awaken by the fierce wind, loud cracks of thunder the sound of doors in the house opening and shutting. He got out of bed and looked past the rain-streaked window to the yard below. There, near the gate, was a faint light. Looking closer he saw the figure of a man with a lantern staring up at the house. Hearing the sound of someone moving around downstairs, George thought it was either Henry White or Moses Polley and went back to bed.

It wasn't long after when he heard pounding on the floor in the rooms below. Then the sound of blows, again and again and again. Twice he heard a startled cry, "Oh!"

Terrified, Bolles hid inside a small blanket trunk in his room, covering his ears to prevent hearing any of the terrible sounds. He stayed there for many hours, paralyzed with fear. Eventually

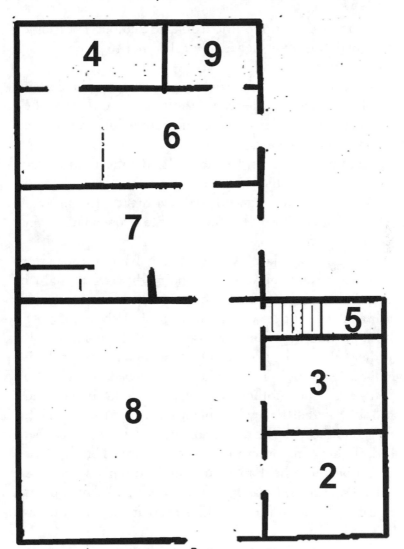

The Crouch home layout.
1: Alcove where Jacob Crouch slept
2: Front bedroom occupied by Mrs. & Mrs. Henry White
3: Bedroom occupied by Moses Polley
4: Bedroom occupied by the housekeeper
5: Stairs leading to upper chambers where Bolles slept
6: Dining room with entrance from east
7: Sitting room
8: Parlor with entrance from the south
9: Pantry

exiting the confined interior of the trunk, he cautiously descended the stairs. There was total silence. He called out to Jacob Crouch several times without response.

Going outside he peaked through an opening in the curtains and saw Mr. Crouch lying peacefully in the alcove. Though he'd seen no evidence of murder, George knew something wasn't right and took off to tell someone.

After alerting Clements, George left to inform Susan and Daniel Holcomb, Jacob's daughter and son-in-law, and his youngest son, Judd Crouch, who lived with the Holcombs. As George headed off, Ray went to check out the Crouch farm. What he found was horrific.

First discovered was Jacob Crouch's body lying in the parlor's alcove, his face toward the wall. Anyone might have thought he was peacefully sleeping if it hadn't been for the blood coating his white hair and beard. There was a bullet hole just above his ear.

With a great sense of unease, Ray reluctantly made his way through the parlor to the bedroom that belonged to Jacob. Inside he found the body of Moses Polley on the bed, a bullet hole through his chest and another by his ear. Blood on the floor near the door told Ray that Polley had likely been shot there, his body later dragged to the bed. The dresser drawers in the room had been ransacked, clothing and other items thrown everywhere.

The next bedroom held an even more disturbing scene. There on the blood soaked bed was Henry White, a bullet hole behind his right ear, a second in the top of his head and a third that had grazed his scalp.

Perhaps most tragic was the body of Eunice White, just a few days from delivering their much anticipated baby. She had obviously been awake and aware of her attacker. Bullet wounds in her arms indicated an attempt to protect herself. Another bullet was found lodged in her neck yet another in her head.

Ray, hearing noises in the kitchen, entered to find the housekeeper, Julia Reese, getting ready to make breakfast. She was completely unaware of what horrors lay in the next rooms. When told, she'd was shocked and claimed she'd heard noting the night before.

Those first at the scene reported an unusual scent, like Chloroform. Though that smell was gone by the time the sheriff arrived, drugs used to sedate the victims was a possibility, though never confirmed.

Another early arrival at the scene was a man named, Hatch. He saw a number of footprints, of varying sizes, surrounding the house. Some were deep-set as though someone had stood outside for a long time.

When Sheriff Winney finally arrived, a few people had already gathered at the farmhouse. He quickly secured the area for the coroner's examination but, by then, some of the evidence had almost certainly been contaminated.

Based upon the number of footprints found and the method of shooting, it was determined more than one person had likely been involved with the murders, possibly three. It was believed that one probably waited outside as a watch while two others handled the murders.

It wasn't long before word got out. Crowds of people gathered, wanting to help or simply to see the dreadful scene. Three days later, the funeral of Jacob was held at his home. Some reports stated more than 1,000 people turned out for the funeral. Carriages and buggies lined the street and sat on Crouch land.

During his life, Jacob had never had a photograph taken of himself. As was common in the Victorian era, a death photo was taken. They placed his body upright in a chair and took the picture later painting in his eyes. Jacob's death photo can be seen here.

After their funerals, a full out search began for the perpetrators of this horrific crime. First suspects were the housekeeper, Julia Reese, and the hired hand, George Bolles. Authorities, couldn't believe the two didn't hear the shootings and the mayhem that must have followed. They were immediately arrested.

This theory of their guilt was later dismissed when, on George Bolles' suggestion, Sheriff Winney and his team returned to the Crouch home and recreated the murder scene, including shooting a gun. In doing this, they discovered the gunshots had likely gone unheard and unrecognized during the thunderous storm of that

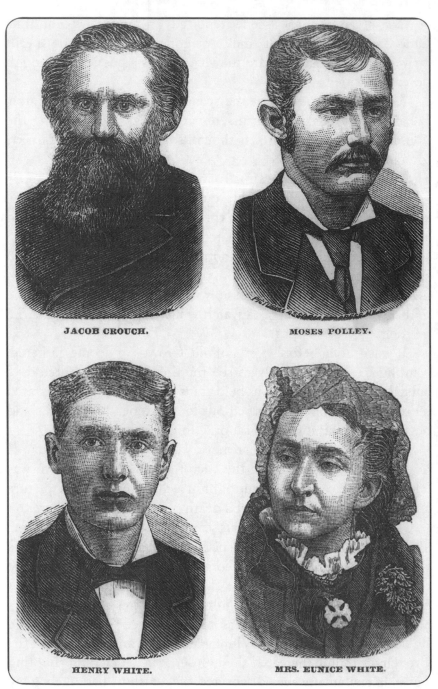

JACOB CROUCH.   MOSES POLLEY.

HENRY WHITE.   MRS. EUNICE WHITE.

evening. Even though they were no longer suspects, Julia and George were held in jail until after the inquest.

What perplexed the police and the prosecutor was identifying a motive. At first they suspected robbery. It was well known that Jacob Crouch kept considerable money at his home and never locked his doors. That idea was dropped when a substantial amount of cash was discovered untouched in the home.

The next possible motive was one of hate. Jacob Crouch was known as a penny-pincher, harsh in manner with a sour disposition. There were many people who had been the subject of Mr. Crouch's rude temper and miserly ways. Unfortunately, most of those leads fell through as well. Suspects came and went.

Sheriff Winney and the team turned their focus to members of the Crouch family, specifically Judd Crouch, Daniel Holcomb, and Daniel's hired hand James Foy. Jacob hadn't held back his disdain for Daniel Holcomb. It is likely the feelings were mutual. Judd Crouch, an outcast of his father since birth, never shared a loving relationship. In fact, many believed Jacob could barely stand to look at his deformed, crippled son. Then there was James Foy. Townspeople looked at him as a disreputable low-life with little moral fiber, capable of almost anything.

As layers of the family's past were revealed, a possible motive arose. It began back in 1859, just a few days after Jacob's youngest son, Judson, was born.

Jacob's wife had a difficult pregnancy and passed away a few days after giving birth to Judd. Sadly, the birth was not a perfect one. Little Judd was born with a deformed, crippled foot. Five or six days later, Jacob gave Judd to Susan and Daniel Holcomb to raise. Susan was Jacob's daughter.

According to Daniel Holcomb, Judd was given to them as a direct request of Jacob's dying wife. Most, however, believed Jacob gave Judd to the Holcombs because he couldn't bear to look at his deformed son whose birth led to his wife's death. Adding to that, Jacob found the idea of raising this handicapped boy too inconvenient. In any event, for the first seven or eight years of his life, Judd believed Susan and Daniel were his parents.

In 1859, when Jacob gave Judd to the Holcombs, some type of monetary compensation for raising the boy was promised. Though Jacob did give Daniel some money over the years, Daniel believed a substantial amount was still owed. This Jacob refused to hand over. The old man's refusal to pay Daniel the additional money was poorly timed with his announced intention of turning over his land and wealth to Eunice and Henry after the birth of their baby.

In that, the police and prosecutor had a motive. Anger, greed and jealousy drove Daniel Holcomb and Judd to murder Jacob, Eunice and Henry White. This would make certain the transfer of wealth did not occur. Moses Polley's death was simply a matter of bad timing. If he hadn't awoken that night, he might have lived. The likelihood of this being the motive became increasingly clear when a small box containing Jacob's stock and land documents was found missing.

The inquest began. Daniel Holcomb and Judd Crouch were the first to be interrogated. Daniel's wife, Susan, was completely overwhelmed by the circumstances. On several occasions she was heard saying the awful death of her father and sister followed so quickly by the accusations against her husband and brother were more than she could bear. Adding to her fears was the thought that her testimony might, in some way, contribute to Daniel's and Judd's conviction.

On the afternoon of January 2, 1884, the Holcomb family returned after Daniel's interrogation to find Susan's bedroom door locked. When they finally got in, they found her lifeless body upon the bed.

A vile of a drug called chlorodyne was found on the dresser and, initially, people thought she had committed suicide. Following that were reports that Daniel may have given her rat poison to keep her from testifying in court.

The autopsy revealed the ultimate cause of death was an enlarged heart. Susan's long-time physician, Dr. Williams, was shocked to learn of her heart condition. She had been his patient for many years and he had not known of her heart trouble. The doctor conjectured it must have advanced rapidly as a result of extreme stress. Susan, in his opinion, had died from a broken heart.

After Susan's death Daniel's brother, Henry Holcomb, and his sister-in-law came from Eaton Rapids to stay with him. Henry Holcomb was a rather bizarre character. Henry appointed himself a detective and, coloring his hair, eyebrows and mustache and donning a pair of weird goggles, went undercover.

In his investigation he identified a man, Joseph Allen, as the Crouch murderer. Based on Henry Holcomb's claims as evidence, Allen was arrested. During trial, it was discovered that Henry Holcomb had perjured himself. Joseph Allen was released and Henry was arrested for perjury. His trial also did not lead to a conviction.

This does not end the story's strange twists and turns. After Susan Holcomb's death, James Foy began to drink heavily. When drunk, he would brag to others about his involvement in the Crouch murders, claiming he was not alone in his deed. He would not, however, reveal the name of his accomplice or accomplices.

In early February 1884, James Foy was found dead at the Jacob Crouch home. He was shot in the head. A pistol was discovered under a hat, at his feet.

Foy's death occurred just moments before the police were to arrest him. It seems he had shot and seriously injured a man he thought was the editor of a Union City newspaper. The editor had written a condemning article about Foy. In it he stated that if Foy was so reticent in telling others about his deed, it was high time the police interrogated him. Not liking this one bit, Foy took revenge and mistakenly shot a man he thought was the editor.

The police were after him. Somehow, Foy made it back to the Crouch farm in a drunken, somber mood swearing he'd kill himself before he let the police arrest him. Judd Crouch, not believing Foy had actually shot someone, left to handle some business in town. That left Mr. and Mrs. Henry Holcomb, Daniel's daughter, Edith, and the elderly Mr. and Mrs. Henry White at the farm. Matthew Brown and his hired hand were also there picking up a load of wheat.

The men were in the barn preparing the wheat when Foy entered. He stayed briefly and, according to testimony, went to the back of the barn where he remained a few minutes before returning to the farmhouse. Moments after entering, the ladies heard a gunshot and found Foy dead.

Suicide was suspected. However, nothing is what it seems in this bizarre story. The autopsy revealed the placement and angle of the wound made it difficult for Foy to fire the gun himself. In addition, there was no gunpowder residue near the wound or on his hat, which would be the case if he had fired the shot himself. Besides that, the gun was found under his hat by his feet. How unlikely would it be for the gun to land under his hat?

Was James Foy murdered and, if so, by whom? Both Dan Holcomb and Judd Crouch had alibis. That left only the ladies and four men as the most likely suspects. Would one or more of those people be capable of killing Foy to stop him from telling the police all that he knew about the murders? A hearing was held but, like so much in this case, remained inconclusive.

Right after the murders, the well-known Pinkerton Detective Agency was brought in, and a substantial reward was offered for anyone who found the murderers. The reward motivated many hopeful, amateur detectives to try their hand at solving the murder and getting the booty. As we've already mentioned, the strange Henry Holcomb, became a self-described detective. Galen Brown, a former police officer from Battle Creek, was another of the self-appointed detectives.

Unlike many of the amateur detectives, Brown had some experience at investigation. Not long before Foy's death, Brown had visited the Crouch farm to interview him. Before leaving, he noticed some papers sticking out of Foy's jacket draped over a chair.

Brown took the papers, later claiming one of them had a most revealing message. It read,

"Judd and Dan, secure those papers. You know only too well what will be done when Eunice's child is born. Foy will assist you in securing them."

Initials underneath the signature read "B.L.C." Brown believed the initial stood for Byron L. Couch, one of Judd's sons who lived in Texas. As it turned out, Byron owed his father a considerable amount of money.

Before he had the chance to give the note to the authorities and just two days after Foy was found dead, Galen Brown was shot point-blank in the chest. While walking down the road, a carriage pulled alongside, a hand reached out with a gun and fired. Galen managed to survive the shooting, later telling the police the man who pulled the trigger was none other than Judd Crouch.

Judd was arrested and brought to trial for Brown's shooting, but charges were dropped when witnesses failed to appear. Even Brown was unable to come to the trial. It seems all of his clothes had been burned and he, quite literally, had nothing to wear. The condemning note, which had been in his pocket at the time of the shooting, disappeared with his clothes.

After the Crouch murders and the deaths of Susan Holcomb and James Foy, Prosecutor Hewlett was certain Judd Crouch and Daniel Holcomb were involved in the crimes. On March 1, 1884, the two men were arrested for the murder of Jacob Crouch, Eunice and Henry White, and Moses Polley. Daniel was the first to go to trial.

November 8, 1884, newspapers across the country called it "The Trial of the Century" and "The Great Trial." People crowded the courtroom with standing room only. Hundreds waited outside the courtroom.

Though the murder weapon was never found, investigators determined a .38 caliber revolver was used. Testimony was given from a Lansing man stating he had sold a .38 caliber gun to Daniel Holcomb. Daniel adamantly denied it, swearing he had never owned such a weapon. After the well-respected Pinkerton Detective Agency came up with proof of its purchase, Daniel relented. He admitted to the Lansing trip and purchase of a .38 caliber revolver but claimed he lost it while hunting in the woods.

Other testimony came from a witness who claimed to have met with James Foy about 10 days before the Crouch murders. According to the witness, Foy confronted him saying:

"You know Mr. Jacob Crouch? Well, he's a damned old hog, and you're just the man I want to help me put him out of the way. He is trying to beat the boys out of their property and we want to save it for them. I can get $2,000 for the job and I'll give you $50 if

you will go out with me right now. I've got a buggy here all ready."
The witness declined and walked away, believing that Foy was not
serious and just shooting-off his mouth.

The witness continued that, after the murders, Foy told him
he should "make himself scarce." Judd and Daniel knew their plan
and would come after him next. The witness left town eventually
returning "out of duty" to tell the Prosecuting Attorney what he
knew.

Galen Brown, somewhat recovered from his wounds, also
contributed testimony. He revealed a conversation with Foy who
claimed two people did the shooting. Foy said he was owed $2,000
by the Crouch estate and that he was afraid Judd and Dan were
going to place the full blame of the murders on him. Foy remained
vague when Galen Brown asked if Judd and Dan took part in the
murders. All Foy told him was, "If worst comes to worst, I can
unravel the whole mystery."

Another bit of interesting testimony came from a young
housekeeper at the Holcomb house. She claimed to have found a
pair of men's pants and a white shirt hidden behind a chest in the
room James Foy and Judd Crouch shared.

According to her testimony, the knees of the pants were saturated
with blood and the shirt had bloodstains above the wristband. She
wasn't certain who the clothing belonged to but recalled Judd
Crouch wearing the same pants a week before. She also testified to
seeing a pair of fine leather boots caked with mud. Because of their
unusual shape, she knew the boots belonged to Judd.

The young woman told the jury she had left the articles of
clothing undisturbed behind the chest. Shortly after she left the
room Judd went inside and removed the clothing and boots. She
never saw them again.

Other condemning testimony was presented. Its importance
was diminished by contradictory rebuttal, a collection of irrelevant
or unreliable witnesses, contaminated evidence and, in the eyes of
the jury, a weak motive. The trial lasted a year. In January of 1885,
the jury came back with a verdict of not guilty. Daniel Holcomb
was free.

Though his uncle's trial was over, Judd Crouch's trial was still pending. Adding even more to Judd's difficulties came in 1886 when a penniless young woman, Jennie Farley, was found dead from an overdose of morphine in a hotel room. She was five or six months pregnant. Jennie had worked as a domestic at Judd's house the summer of 1883 and, since that time, had been seen with him many times.

She was known as "Judd's girl," and most people in town believed he was father of the baby and suspect in the death. He vehemently denied both claims. He was called to give testimony in Jennie Farley's trial and, at its conclusion, was absolved of guilt, her death deemed a suicide. Though Judd was cleared from direct involvement, most still believed he was the father of unborn child and ultimate cause of her death.

Court proceedings for Judd in the Crouch murders remained in limbo for several years. During that time, prosecution hoped to gather more evidence.

In 1886, three bloody shirts were discovered stuffed in a tree stump on the Holcomb property. It was thought the perpetrators of the Crouch murders wore the shirts. A letter "F" was embroidered on one. Some believed the "F" stood for Foy. If that could be proven, it would throw direct suspicion to Judd Crouch because of his close relationship with Foy. Unfortunately, the connection was not made and led nowhere. After exhausting all options, charges were finally dropped in 1891. Judd never went to trial.

Sometime in 1888 Judd married. He left Spring Arbor to settle down in Jackson County and lived a simple but relatively happy life to his death in 1946. Family members say that, in the last moments of his life, he continued to swear his innocence.

Daniel's Holcomb's life after his acquittal was strange. Amanda Crouch, a relative of the Jacob Crouch family, lived in Jackson with her veterinarian husband, Dr. J. S. Baker. At some point, Amanda divorced J.S. and struck up a friendship with Daniel Holcomb.

Though Amanda was twenty years younger than Daniel, a romantic relationship began, and on April 8, 1886, the two were married in Baraboo, Wisconsin. All went well for the next fourteen years. Daniel made a good living in the cattle business and the couple seemed content.

Daniel's strange dreams began in early November 1900. As a friend reported, Daniel told him of recurring nightmares in which he fell from a cliff and drowned in the Wisconsin River. On November 14, 1900, nearly seven years to the day of the Crouch murders, Daniel Holcomb went missing.

He was on a business trip to purchase cattle. The man he was to meet was delayed. Daniel decided to go fishing until the man returned. As fate would have it, the Wisconsin River ran through the farmer's property. Daniel went off with fishing gear and never returned.

A search party discovered footprints near a dangerous ledge on the Wisconsin River. Fingerprints along the edge were believed to be Daniel's final, desperate attempt to save his life before plunging to his death. Though his body wasn't found, his friends and family believed he had died.

That would change a few days later when reports surfaced of Daniel being spotted crossing the Wisconsin River in a skiff. His footprints were tracked through a swamp. He was last seen boarding a train headed west. After that, all trace of Daniel Holcomb was lost.

Nearly one year later, November 11, 1901, Daniel turned up at his daughter's home in Chicago. He claimed to have no recollection of the past year. No one really knows what he had done or where he'd gone. Daniel returned with his wife, Amanda, to their Baraboo, Wisconsin, home.

December 7, 1903, approximately two years after Daniel's return, Amanda unexpectedly died. As of this writing, we have been unable to determine her cause of death. Though pure conjecture on our part, we can't help but wonder if Daniel had a hand in her early demise. After her death, Daniel led a quiet life finally passing away in 1920.

According to the Kalamazoo Gazette, sometime on or before 1899 the old Jacob Crouch property was divided, sold to others and the farmhouse torn down. Now, some may think that ends the strange series of events surrounding this story. Not quite. In 1919 it was discovered all court records related to the Crouch murders had vanished. It is not known when they disappeared or how it happened.

Everyone and everything related to the horrific murders of November 21-22, 1883, are now gone. All that is left are the stories and, of course, the urban legend.

Eunice was a favored child and closest to her father's heart. She, in turn, loved her ornery old father. For all of his harsh words and penny-pinching ways Eunice knew his softer side. A side few others saw.

As the legend goes, on the anniversary of their deaths Eunice's spirit leaves her grave at St. John's Cemetery and travels to Reynolds Cemetery to reunite with the spirit of her beloved father, Jacob. It is said if you visit Reynolds Cemetery on the anniversary of their deaths, you will see the mist carrying the spirit of Eunice to Jacob.

For some, this is where the story of the Crouch murders ends. For us, it is the beginning.

Where this story will take us is a multi-site paranormal investigation beginning at the graves of Jacob Crouch and Susan Holcomb at Reynolds Cemetery. The next stop would be St. John's and Woodland Cemeteries, where Eunice and Henry White and Judd Crouch were buried. The investigation would wrap up with a hunt at the scene of the murders, the old Jacob Crouch farm. Would we be able to collect audio, video or photographic evidence that might provide answers to these unsolved murders?

Our fascination with this case began with Jeff Westover, a colleague who also happens to be an incredible photographer and author of a soon-to-be released book, "Ghost Highways" www.ghost-highway.com. His unique book will be a fascinating compilation of experimental photography focused on historical places, some of which are said to be haunted.

During a conversation, Jeff eagerly shared a recent experience while photographing Reynolds Cemetery. He arrived one morning just after the cemetery opened. Alone in the quiet morning, the only sounds were the soft, lamenting call of mourning doves.

As is Jeff's custom, he brought an audio recorder during his photographic shoot. While standing near Susan Holcomb's grave, he asked a few questions. Not hearing anything, he completed his photography session and went home.

Later, when listening to the audio, Jeff was surprised to find something very interesting had been recorded. Bev and I were more than a little intrigued when we heard Jeff's EVP. It was this important audio clip that began our journey into the Crouch saga.

Investigating the cemeteries would be easy. Getting permission to investigate the old Crouch farm would not. We were very happy when Jeff connected us with Sean and Beth Campbell, founders of Campbell Paranormal Investigations who knew the current owners, J.R. and Jules. After a brief chat with J.R., he agreed to take us out to the farm. Sean Campbell would join us for that portion of the investigation. For now, however, we were ready to begin the cemetery investigations with Jeff.

Bev and I are not of the belief that a paranormal investigation must always be conducted late at night. In fact, for cemetery hunts we prefer to investigate during the day when visibility is good and a headstone, tree or shrub doesn't look like a ghostly apparition. Of course, there are challenges with daytime cemetery hunts. Voices of other, living visitors can be picked up as EVPs. Adding to the challenge is the sound of traffic and wind, which is usually more prevalent during the day.

In this case, we really didn't have a choice. Jackson County enforces strict laws prohibiting nighttime cemetery investigations. They do not bend the rules for anyone. Not wanting the wrath of Jackson County's finest and preferring not to wear clothes with the words Jackson Prison on the back, we chose the daytime to investigate.

The day of the cemetery investigation was a beautiful, unusually warm spring day. Though a deep blue sky, puffs of white clouds and a calm wind did not have the creepy effect of dark night, the warmth was still very welcomed.

Bev and I arrived at Reynolds Cemetery before Jeff Westover and decided to check it out. Reynolds is a small, very historic

Courtesy of Jeff Westover

It is believed Jacob Crouch rests under the flat stone in the photo's forefront.

place. Many of Jackson County's earliest pioneers are buried here. Located in a country setting, there are not many businesses or residential homes nearby. It is, however, on a relatively busy intersection. Though periodic cars and trucks rumbled by it wasn't heavy enough to completely prohibit a daytime investigation.

There are several Crouch and Holcomb grave sites at Reynolds. Susan Holcomb's grave is at the back. Though the exact location of Jacob's grave is unknown, his gravestone removed or stolen some years back, it is thought to be close to the front, near other Crouch tombstones.

While Bev went off to get some photographs, I moved to the Holcomb grave site. Pulling out my video camera, I mindlessly turned it on and pressed record. The LCD screen flooded pure white. Thinking it had been left in night-vision, I flipped the switch to daytime mode. No change.

I reset the camera, removed and replaced batteries. No luck. The darned camera was stuck on nightvision. It was impossible to record in daylight. I've had this camera for two years and never had a problem.

Well, no panic, I thought. Bev had brought the back-up video camera. I went to our gear bag, pulled it out and clicked-in the fresh battery, switched it on and waited. Nothing.

This was ridiculous! Looking around I noted the electric wire poles in the back and wondered if they may be generating unusually high EMF, which could affect the equipment. After walking the length of the yard, however, I found levels to be completely normal.

As a last alternative, I went for my still camera. The video mode on my still camera works fine in daylight. I fished it out of my gear bag and turned it to video mode. It ran maybe a second then stopped. The rear digital screen flashed internal error. What the...

I pulled out the memory card and put it back. Turned the camera on and off. Same error. Good gravy! As a last resort and the only logical approach to digital equipment repair, I began to violently shake it. Bev came over.

"What in the world are you doing?"

"Fixing this friggin' camera!" When the shaking failed, I put the whole mess of useless equipment in my gear bag and pulled out my trusty digital audio recorder.

"Is your equipment working OK?"

Bev looked down at her camera, clicked off a few shots, looked at me and smiled. Good gravy.

I turned on the audio recorder. The battery was almost dead.

Bev laughed, "Geesh, you sure didn't come very prepared."

"I charged everything this morning and replaced batteries! I'm getting crazy internal errors and equipment malfunctions. It all worked fine this morning. There's some bad ju-ju here."

"Mm-hmm. The only bad ju-ju is you."

Waving her off, I made my way back to the car for more batteries. Fortunately, fresh ones did the trick and within moments the digital recorder was up and running. We both returned to the area where Jacob Crouch's grave site was said to be.

"Mr. Crouch, are you here? Can you tell us who killed you on that stormy November evening?" All was quiet except for a sudden rush of wind across the graveyard. It swirled around us before dissipating.

After several moments, we walked to the Holcomb grave site. "Susan, did you really kill yourself?"

That's when we heard the crunch of tires on gravel. Jeff had arrived. After greetings, he handed us a folder nearly an inch thick. It contained copies of all the newspaper articles he'd collected during his research.

In addition to his own research, Jeff had gathered additional information from Janine Turvey and Gerry Blanchard, two people who have spent years investigating the murders. Though we have conducted our own research into this case, Jeff's knowledge was incredibly useful. It was also very kind of Jeff to share his files with us.

Jeff Westover has done extensive research on the Crouch Murders

As the three of us assembled near Susan Holcomb's grave, we asked Jeff to tell us about the Crouch murders. Bev and I have found talking about the event or time period surrounding the haunting can stir up paranormal activity. With our invitation, Jeff shared some of what he knew about the murders. When he was finished, we all stood in silence listening and watching.

I asked Susan or any of the Holcomb spirits if Daniel had done something to prevent Jacob's money from going to Eunice. The question seemed to go unanswered.

A strange look passed across Jeff's face. He pointed to the sloping grounds and electrical lines, "I often get … and I'm feeling it now … a sense of dizziness in here, but those lines do put off high EMF."

I took out my EMF reader and again moved to the electric lines. Just like before, levels remained very low. If Jeff had found high EMF readings before, today that was not the case. They were completely normal. Whatever was causing Jeff's sudden dizziness had nothing to do with high EMF.

We continued with EVP questions, addressing Daniel Holcomb's parents. Bev and I both noticed the sudden breeze as the names were spoken, "Henry Holcomb or would Jane Holcomb be here?" The breeze slowly stilled leaving nothing but the soft chirping of birds.

Nearly an hour passed. Traffic on the crossroads was increasing and the noise became a problem. We moved on to St. John's and Woodland Cemeteries, about five or six miles away.

These two locations are connected forming one, very large cemetery. The Catholic section is called St. John's. Eunice and Henry White are buried there. Judd Crouch's grave site lies somewhere in the neighboring Woodland Cemetery.

"Assassinated." That's what the inscription read on Eunice and Wm. Henry White's tombstones. It was a powerful moment. Though there were two tombstones, we knew a third soul was with them, their unborn baby. The memorial stone marked "White" sat in front of their gravestones. On it was an inscription, which Jeff began to read:

"William H. White and Eunice, his wife, assassinated on the night of November 21, 1883 … how well prepared for the swift approaching shock. Although unwarned we mourn …"

Jeff stopped unable to see the remaining worn, aged words. Bev brought water. Wetting the stone improved its legibility and, this time, Bev continued reading:

"How pure those hearts how well prepared for the swift approaching shock. Although unwarned we know their hopes… were founded on the rock. Fate shows our treasures, father's sons,

Eunice and William White and their unborn child.

where hearts may trust their prize. Rest in homes not made with hands, eternal in the skies. But the Good Sheppard watched his own, his power out sped the blow. The stricken lambs lay on His breast are loved, are safe we know."

After she finished, the three of us stood in respectful silence. Bev and I glanced at each other, silently acknowledging the returning wind as she finished reading the inscription on the tombstone.

The three of us directed our series of questions to Eunice and Henry White. The questions were similar to what we'd asked near Jacob's and Susan's graves. Who was the murderer? Was there more than one person who did the shooting? The sound of birds and children playing in the distance did little to lessen the intensity of anticipation. This uncanny feeling remained throughout our time at the Holcomb grave site, though nothing remotely unusual was heard or felt.

It was getting late. Bev, Jeff and I proceeded with our last stop, Judd Crouch's grave. Not sure where it was, we spread out to begin the search. Finding the site would be a little like finding a needle in a haystack. Woodland Cemetery is quite a large place. Slowly walking, eyes scanning the surrounding gravestone.

Come on Judd, I thought, help me out here. Where are you? It was then, either by coincidence or spectral direction, that I found myself standing directly in front of the small headstone marked J.D. Crouch. The timing was short of remarkable.

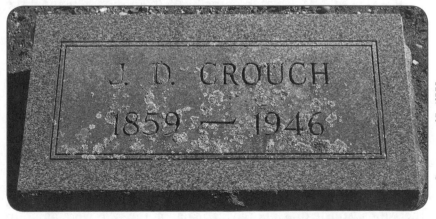

In such a large cemetery, what drew Kat to Judd's tombstone?

After signaling to the others, I returned to the headstone and stared down at the dates 1859 to 1946. Whatever Judd did or didn't do, he certainly lived a long life. Next to his grave was another. The name on it was Viola Crouch, his wife. They married in 1888, had one child, Ruth, and remained together until her death in 1942.

From what Bev and I read on genealogy blogs, Judd was a loving husband and father. Some believed his wife, Viola, was the first person to truly love him. He was close to family members as well. Friendly and cheerful, he often attended reunions and, to his dying day, continued to profess his innocence.

His grave site was in a quiet section of the cemetery, away from most of the traffic noise. A particularly peaceful location with a scattering of tall, mature trees and gently rolling grounds. It was curious that, with all the beautiful trees in the cemetery, the one near Judd's grave was completely opposite. Short, rather grotesque yet imposing, its thick branches bent and twisted, deformed. Very much like Judd.

One newspaper article had described him as a sturdy young man with a hunched back and deformed, twisted foot. It was fitting, perhaps, that he would be buried near this old tree so out of place with the others.

Bev and Jeff had joined me at the grave site. The air was deadly still as I began my question. "Judd Crouch, were you involved with the murder of your father, and Eunice, and William?"

It was peculiar; with each name I called out the intensity of the wind increased. Of course wind is unpredictable. Its coincidental occurrence did not likely signify a paranormal event. Yet, we couldn't help wonder if there was some significance in its timely appearance throughout the afternoon.

I continued, "For once you can tell us, Judd, how you were involved or if you were involved with your family's murder."

Jeff took his turn. "Judd, my name's Jeff; I've been talking to Susan, Jacob, and Eunice. Now's the chance for you to say your peace. I've spoken with them. It's your turn. We need for you to talk. You need to tell us what you know. Who killed your family?" The winds vanished as quickly as it had come. We were alone in the warm spring sun.

It was late afternoon as our trio headed back. Though nothing obvious had occurred this day, we remained hopeful something would turn up during analysis.

A week passed and our on-site investigation of the Crouch homestead approached. The night before, it stormed, eerily reminiscent of the night before the Crouch murders. Heavy winds, thunder, rain and hail the size of big, fat grapes pelted the ground. Electricity was knocked out, a few homes and cars had been damaged. Though the severe weather was over as we made our way to Spring Arbor, the rain still fell in a steady sheet.

It was just after 6:00 P.M. when we met J.W. and Sean in the parking lot of Reynolds Cemetery. After our greetings, J.W. went on to the property while Sean, Bev and I made a brief stop at Reynolds. The video cameras that malfunctioned during our last visit were at the repair shop. I had a new video camera today and, hopefully, no equipment problems.

Our feet scuffed through the puddles of water and wet grass as the three of us wandered through the old cemetery. I ran a short EVP session and was thrilled when my new video camera functioned flawlessly.

During this visit, the cemetery had a different feel, not just because of the rain. Its atmosphere was more charged… more alive. Within a short time the three of us were drenched, the rain coming down in torrents. Cutting our EVP session short, we returned to the protection of the cars and followed Sean Campbell to the Crouch farm.

We are purposefully not disclosing the exact location of the Crouch farm based on the current owners' request. We can say it wasn't far from Reynolds Cemetery.

How understated the land appeared. A small home, on a quiet country road, partially hidden behind a cluster of trees. It wasn't the original Crouch home, of course. That had been taken down long ago. This one had been built sometime around 1947 or 1948. A portion of the house did sit on the original home's foundation.

To the back of the land was an ancient barn, a tall silo standing almost protectively in front. We met up again with J.W. who confirmed that, to the best of his knowledge, the barn was original.

The current home resting on the Crouch property.

He then took us to meet his wife, Jules. Both were incredibly friendly and welcoming, especially under such rainy, bleak conditions.

With them this evening was Scott, a colleague of theirs, and Randy Waltz. Randy is another person who has spent several years researching the Crouch murders. He provided further insight into the unsolved case. Based on his research and personal feelings, he believed Henry Holcomb, Daniel Holcomb's brother, may have murdered James Foy so he wouldn't tell police about the murders. It made sense.

With the rain nearly stopped and darkness beginning to settle in, J.W. took us to the barn. Gray skies were visible through the broken, weather-ravaged roof. Hollow sounds followed us as footsteps echoed off aged walls. We scuffed across the floor cluttered with remnants of hay, leaves and scattered debris. Stalls stood on the left and an old ladder angled upward to a top loft.

At one point in the early Crouch investigation, it was believed the body of a man had been found in the hayloft. That was determined to be a false rumor. The barn was also the place where the ravaged, blood-soaked clothes, mattresses, and sheets from the murders were stored in the days following the tragic event. For that reason, the barn became a very popular location for morbid curiosity seekers.

This very old barn is believed to be the original built by Jacob Crouch

We made our way to the center of the room and quietly took in the surroundings. Though portions of the barn were newer, perhaps updated in the 1940s or 1950s, it was obvious much of the original remained.

Bev began the questions. As she did, coolness slowly crept through the open doors and squeezed through cracks in the walls and frail roof. I involuntarily shivered, drawing my rain-soaked coat closer.

"Daniel Holcomb, are you here?"

The rain begin again. Light taps whispered on the roof. At first we thought they were a response to our questions, but it soon became apparent it was just rain.

Bev continued her slow series of questions. "Did you hide in here and wait for the Crouches? How long did you wait? Did you kill them?"

The rain picked up, its strength creating a riotous echo in the empty room. We glanced at each other with a grimace. The likelihood of collecting EVPs was impossible. Reluctantly we made our way through the pouring rain back to the others who were huddled in the home's back sunroom. Though it was not the Crouch farmhouse, it is possible the home still held some of the original spirit energy. We could check it out next.

The murderers may have hidden in the barn that fateful night.

The group greeted us with big smiles as we entered and laughed as we boldly revealed our wind- and rain-ravaged hair-dos. Really, Bev and I couldn't have been any wetter if we had jumped in the lake. Of course, when you're this wet, getting wetter really doesn't matter. So, when Randy asked if we'd like to see where the original foundations of the home lay, Bev and I followed him back outside.

Returning to the front, he pointed to a slight elevation in the land and the remnants of rocks partially buried in the ground. These aged rocks had likely formed the original farmhouse foundation. Bev and I stepped onto the elevation which had likely been the front of the Crouch home. I recalled an old newspaper article saying Jacob Crouch's body had been lying in an alcove in the front of the home. Perhaps this was the very area in which we now stood.

I felt a cool breeze and, at the same time an unexpected, dull pain on my chest as though I'd been hit with something. The breeze certainly hadn't been strong enough to do that, and I wasn't aware of an object striking me. The pain quickly subsided, it seemed relatively unimportant at the time and was quickly forgotten. The next morning, however, I would find a rather painful bruise. What is even more bizarre, the bruise was in such a position that, if it had been caused by a bullet, would have pierced my heart.

As the evening progressed, Sean Campbell joined Bev and I as we began our investigation of the house. A narrow stairway took us to the basement. With a high ceiling and cinderblock walls, we could tell it was a relatively new construction. To be honest, as creepy as most basements are, this area felt rather benign. We ran a short EVP session before heading back upstairs.

Sean Campbell, from Campbell Paranormal Investigations, waiting for a response in the basement.

Remnants of old cabinets and countertops remained in the old country kitchen reflecting the style of the late 1940s. Continuing through the small area, we entered a slightly larger room with other adjoining rooms. One to the left and back, the others to our right. Rooms had been gutted with some signs of new construction.

We ascended the stairs to the second floor where J.R. gave us a quick tour before leaving us. Sean and I settled in for an EVP session while Bev returned to the first floor wanting to run a private EVP session. Walking into a side room at the front of the house and she sat down. The rain had slowed to a gentle shower as her questions began.

"Why do you stay here? Why haven't you gone to rest?" That's when she heard a sound, raspy, hollow, almost mechanical. Yet, there was something human about it. The words eluded her at the time but little did she realize how important their meaning would be.

"Are you waiting for the murderer to return?" No sound or voices this time but the room was filled with an intensity that, for the first time, made Bev feel uneasy. A faint, hazy light filtered in from the open window. Enough light for her to see there was no one in the room with her; yet, Bev knew she was not alone.

"Why do you stay here?" She whispered. That's when the second response came.

After an uneventful session upstairs, Sean and I returned to the first floor. Bev stood in the front room with J.R. chatting. Bev glanced at me and I could tell something had happened. When I asked, she just shrugged her shoulders.

J.R. eventually waved us into a small room at the front of the house. Unknown to our group at the time, it was the same room Bev had been in during her private EVP session. J.R. explained it was in this room a friend had gotten a response when she had called the name of Jacob's youngest daughter, Eunice.

J.R. invited us to stay for a while and enjoy our "EVP-ing", as he jokingly calls it. Leaving, he pointed to a heap of scrap metal on the floor and told us if we wanted to move it aside for him that would be fine. We gazed, in trepidation, at the size and weight of the metal realizing what a great sense of humor J.R. has.

Taking our positions in the room, Sean, Bev and I began another EVP session. We asked what had become a common series of questions… was Daniel or Judd involved with the murders. No obvious response or unusual EMF spikes were detected.

Who remains in this room where EVPs were collected?

We had taken up enough of J.R.'s, Jules' and Sean's time, and we decided to leave. Bev and I enjoyed meeting J.R. and Jules and truly appreciated their permitting access to investigate this historic property. They had all been incredibly patient and accommodating throughout the entire lengthy and very wet process.

We got into the car and quickly turned the heater to high. Ah, thank goodness for modern-day inventions. We may still have been drenched but we were at least warm. As we made our way back home, Bev shared her experience in the back room, which made both of us eager to begin the audio analysis.

Now for the evidence, we'll get right down to it. Wind was a real problem throughout the investigation. It contaminated some of the audio but certainly not all of it.

The first recorded EVP occurred while Bev and I were waiting for Jeff at Reynolds Cemetery. It said, "Something's under the car." What that something was remains unknown, though I wonder if it was the bad ju-ju that caused my video equipment to malfunction.

Next was audio recorded near Susan Holcomb's grave site. I asked if she'd really killed herself. The response sounded very much like, "No, dumb poor girl."

In the same location, Jeff was explaining Daniel's motive for wanting the death of his father and sister, I had asked, "Daniel, did you try and do anything to prevent Jacob from giving the money to Eunice?" Jeff's audio picked up a clear, "Yes."

It's interesting that Daniel's grave is not in the Holcomb family plot. He is buried with his wife, Amanda, in Baraboo, Wisconsin. Yes there was still a response. Though buried in Wisconsin, it is possible Daniel's spirit remains with Susan, his son and parents at Reynolds Cemetery?

There were other interesting EVPs captured at Reynolds, which can be heard in our Web site's Secret Room.

Unfortunately, the wind was a problem for the St. John's and Woodland investigations. Most of the audio was contaminated. In spite of that, we did find a few revealing and surprising audio responses.

At St. John's Cemetery, we asked Eunice and her husband, William Henry, if there had been one or two murderers; the response was, "Get it straight." Seems the spirits were chastising us for not knowing the facts.

Another EVP was recorded on Jeff's recorder near Judd's grave. I asked, "Do you know who killed your family?" The simple response was, "Yes."

Again, at Judd's grave site, I asked if he had killed Jacob, Eunice and William (William Henry Holcomb), the wind had picked up with each name called out. What Bev and I discovered in analysis was the sound of spoken words buried within the sound of wind. The words were certainly not ours. After cleaning the audio, the words we believe it says, "I think I did." This is rather perplexing. Wouldn't Judd know for certain if he had or had not committed the murders? You can hear this audio clip in our Web site.

More audio evidence was captured in the barn. When asked if Daniel Holcomb was present in the barn, the EVP came back, "Yes." Also captured was a second name. Though soft, we believe it says, "Henry Holcomb." Henry, of course, was Daniel Holcomb's brother and a possible suspect in the murder of James Foy.

When asked who the murderer was, the response was, "Too many." This seems to support the theory that many conspirators were involved with the killings.

Interesting EVPs were captured in or near the home. While walking outside the house, I called the name of Eunice White. "Help me," was heard. Inside the home, an audio recorder had been placed on a ledge near the kitchen. The soft words, "It's him," followed by a clear, "papa."

Another interesting and perhaps revealing audio was captured in the house. I asked what happened the night of the murders. The soft replay is believed to say, "They came at night," or, "Two men at night." You can listen to this EVP and many others in our Secret Room and decide for yourself.

During Bev's private EVP session on the first floor of the home, one of the questions asked was, "Are you waiting for the murderer to return?" A second of silence, then the word, "Mercy!" Was it the last plea from Eunice, before the final shot ending her life?

The next question was directed to Eunice, "Did you throw your arms up to try and protect yourself." A very soft response followed, "Help."

Bev and I were incredibly surprised at the amount of audio evidence collected during this series of investigations. However, did we collect evidence that may reveal the name or names of the guilty? Yes.

It begins with the EVP session Sean, Bev and I conducted at the end of our investigation in the home. We were in the side room of the main floor.

"Was Daniel involved?" I asked.

"Yes."

"Was Judd involved?"

"Yes."

"Did you see James Foy?"

"No."

Further responses to Bev's questions would reveal more. Following the question, "Why do you stay here?" The response, "Judd's the killer."

Of all the EVPs recorded, however, the most revealing and surprising comes from our friend Jeff Westover. These are the EVPs that started us on this fascinating journey.

The first was recorded in the early morning hours at Reynolds Cemetery. Jeff asks, "If anyone wants to tell me who the murderer was of the Crouch family, please tell me now." The clear, unequivocal response, "Danny."

The second audio clip Jeff sent was also recorded at Reynolds Cemetery. Knowing that Jacob enjoyed drinking, Jeff loudly called out, "Drinks are on Jacob!" Jeff told us to listen just before he speaks. A single word, "Dan" was clearly heard. There was no question about it.

Upon our closer analysis, however, there seemed to be a continuation after Jeff spoke. We removed Jeff's words and clipped the two audio pieces together? The EVP was clear and its meaning unquestionable.

"Dan shot us."

Have the spirits of those who have passed finally given us the answer to this 130-year-old murder mystery? If we believe this, then the final pieces of the puzzle have come together.

Daniel Holcomb fired the fatal shots that stormy November evening. Judd Crouch, if he wasn't one of the shooters, at least played a major role in the murders. For all that James Foy talked about being the killer, the EVP responses seem to indicate he was more likely a key conspirator and may have been the man standing watch. Though not seen by the victims, Foy was still a part of the murders.

There is still at least one answered question. Did James Foy actually kill himself or was he murdered? If murdered, by whom? Ah, but that is another investigation for another time.

For now, we hope the tormented souls of those involved can finally rest. But then perhaps not all can rest or should rest. The final EVP is prophetic. Recorded by Bev during her private EVP session in the home, she asked, "Why haven't you gone to rest?" The quiet raspy breath responded, "Murderers don't sleep."

Story Four
Seul Choix Point Lighthouse

672 N. West Gulliver Lake Road, Gulliver, MI
Password: scp2009
Investigative Team:
Upper Peninsula Paranormal Research Society (UPPRS)
Historical Assistance: Val Wheatley

Kat and I were heading to Gulliver in Michigan's Upper Peninsula. We love the U.P. and were looking forward to this road trip. Our destination was the Seul Choix Point Lighthouse.

The name Seul Choix is French and means "only choice." When the French and Native Americans traveled across Lake Michigan's northern shores, the point was the only safe harbor for boats to land in a storm. The name Seul Choix is pronounced "Sel-shwa" by the French, but locals used the term "Sis-shwa."

There are rumors it is haunted by a former lighthouse keeper, Captain Joseph Willie Townshend. We hoped to find out during our investigation.

It was just a six-hour drive from the Detroit area. Not too far for a nice long weekend in the glorious north. Our car was packed with all the necessities, including 39 bottles of water. That way we could stop and visit the many beautiful rest areas along I-75.

Starting out Kat had her video camera ready for any wild animals that may cross our path. I explained we were still in her driveway and she could rest for a few miles.

Several hours later we were approaching the magnificent Mackinac Bridge. Kat's left hand reached for the video camera, while her right hand pushed the down button of her window. Kat's #1 rule on the bridge is to roll down the windows of our little car in case it's blown off the bridge. According to Kat, this will enable us to escape so we can swim to safety. I've never told her swimming to safety is not an option, so we continue to roll down our windows.

It was about midday as our car pulled onto the road leading to Seul Choix. Suddenly we were surrounded by dense woods and isolated from the rest of the world. As remote as it was now, we wondered what it might have been like more than 100 years ago.

Continuing along this lonely road, there was movement in the trees. A family of deer appeared. Kat turned on her video camera and captured the deer as they took a leisurely stroll across the dirt road. I asked if she got them. In disgust she replied, "Through the bug splattered window. Maybe we'll spot them again when we get to the on top of the lighthouse."

I agreed, "That would be an awesome shot."

Through the trees the imposing tower of Seul Choix Point Lighthouse appeared. Surrounded by deep blue sky and puffs of white clouds, it was a photographer's dream. It looked pretty darn good considering it was built in 1895.

We would be joining Upper Peninsula Paranormal Research Society (UPPRS), for this investigation. UPPRS is a well-known group in the Mid West and a TAPS family member. Its founder and field director is Tim Ellis. Upon arrival, Tim introduced us to Brad Blair, historian and lead investigator as well as the other team members, Lance, Matt, Michelle and Ryan. They were already busy unpacking equipment.

Entering the keeper's quarters, we found ourselves in a small parlor, surrounded by the past. An antique piano sat against one wall, covered with a collection of photographs of past light keepers and their families.

Three ladies sat in the room chatting. One of them stood to greet us, introducing herself as Marilyn Fischer, President of the Gulliver Historical Society. Joining her was Shirley Wardwell, Vice President of the Historical Society and Polly Merrell, lighthouse tour guide.

These ladies and others from the Seul Choix Historical Society have done an outstanding job of maintaining one of Upper Michigan's most historic and beautiful lighthouses. It's through dedicated people like Marilyn, Shirley and Polly that our state's past is kept alive. We want to thank all of those who volunteer their time to support such a worthwhile cause.

After getting acquainted we invited the ladies to share their stories of ghostly activities. They were happy to do so.

According to Marilyn the most common occurrences are cold spots and unusual smells, especially the pungent odor of cigar smoke. She equates the cigar smoke to Captain Joseph "Willie" Townshend, the second lighthouse keeper and resident spirit. It seems the captain loved cigars, but his wife forbid him to smoke in the house. Now his spirit smokes indoors whenever he chooses.

One area of paranormal activity surrounds the table in the original kitchen. It is the only piece of original furniture and was discovered in the basement several years ago. Once it was brought

Marilyn Fischer, President of the Gulliver Historical Society, explains why she believes Captain Joseph Townshend remains at the lighthouse.

up and put together, things began to happen. People have heard the sound of the table moving and noticed silverware askew.

A dark mist, shaped like a raven, is often sighted floating across the dining room ceiling. This room contains a Bible where the pages are known to turn when no one is around.

There are accounts of a man with a bushy, white beard being seen. Based on the description, Marilyn believes it is Captain Townshend. The captain has been seen on the main floor and also spotted staring out an upper floor window.

"It's like a portal from the other side." That's how Marilyn describes the mirror in a second floor bedroom where she believes the spirits in the home come and go. On several occasions she has seen the apparitions of two women. Marilyn believes one of them is Grandma Pemble, mother-in-law of a past light keeper. There were many other bizarre stories too numerous to recount.

Kat and I believe the more we know about people from the past, the easier it becomes to understand a haunting. With Marilyn's vast knowledge, the assistance of historian Vel Wheatley, and our own research, we have come to understand the life and hardships of the Seul Choix Point keepers and their families.

The lighthouse was placed into service in 1892 but, because of construction problems, wasn't completed until 1895. Overall, the tower stands more than 78 feet with 96 steps. Lighthouse keepers needed good legs for the numerous trips up the stairs each day.

The very first lighthouse keeper was a man by the name of Captain Joseph Fountain, part Chippewa Indian, who managed from 1892 till 1901. For nearly twenty years he dedicated himself to the lighthouse.

An example of his extreme dedication came in September 1894. One night during a fierce storm, the schooner William Home sank just off Seul Choix Point. Massive whitecaps and blinding winds made it treacherous for Captain Fountain as he searched for possible survivors. Ready to give up, his eyes roamed the waters one last time. He saw the only survivor floating ashore, unconscious on a piece of yawl boat. Sadly the body of a woman was found about the same time not far away. Captain Fountain brought the survivor back to the house to recover.

The next lighthouse keeper, from 1901 to 1910, was Captain Joseph Willie Townshend. He lived there with his second wife and three children. Eventually his son, Ivan, would become an assistant keeper.

The Captain was a very stern taskmaster and not well loved by his assistants. He could often be heard snapping out orders to his men. On August 10, 1910, Captain Townshend died, some believe from lung cancer. His death certificate, however, lists cause of death as chronic bronchitis, with senility as a contributing factor. If this is true, the captain's senility could have been the cause of his anger and harshness in later years.

There are rumors that Captain Townshend was hated by his staff and, after he died, was beaten. There is also talk that he may not have been dead when the beating started. We could find no evidence to support these claims. Whatever happened, it seems certain that Townshend's last days were confusing and difficult. Marilyn tells us he was embalmed in the basement and laid out in the home until family members from other locations arrived.

After Joseph Townshend's passing, his son Ivan continued to serve the lighthouse as an assistant. As fate would have it, just two years later, Ivan and his wife faced yet another painful tragedy. Their two-year-old daughter, Margaret, contracted diphtheria and eventually passed away. The loss of their little girl would stay with them the rest of their lives.

Interestingly, William Blanchard, a lighthouse assistant, and not Ivan Townshend would succeed Captain Townshend as keeper. William would hold this position for the next 31 years. While working there he met and married Amanda Pemble

Of course, life at the lighthouse wasn't all work. William and Amanda enjoyed a little free time and were known to break up the hard, tedious routine with a little fun.

As the daughter of an assistant light keeper recounts, the Blanchards would sometimes pull back the furniture in the parlor, turn on the Edison Reel Phonograph, and have a little square dance party. It was a time everyone at the lighthouse enjoyed.

Amanda Blanchard was a loving, nurturing woman who cared for her family. She also served as midwife for many of the women in the community. In 1912, William and Amanda began their own family and, by 1917, had two little boys, five and three years old. Things were going pretty well for the Blanchards until Amanda received word that her mother, Mary Pemble, had taken ill.

Mary, living a few miles away in Mackinac County, was very close to Amanda, William and the

Amanda Blanchard (L) with her mother, Mary "Grandma" Pemble (R)

Courtesy Gulliver Historical Society

boys. She was known by most simply as Grandma Pemble. In 1917 at the age of 57 Mary Pemble became ill. The family was especially shaken when they learned Grandma Pemble's illness was the worst of all possible conditions, cancer.

In those days there was little chance of survival from this hideous disease. Surgery, though very risky for patients, was the only possible option for Mary. Even though it would only extend her life one to three years, she chose surgery.

At some point during this period, she came to live with the Blanchard family; after all, Amanda did have some medical experience as a mid-wife. Mary was a strong woman with a strong will, but it seemed the disease was stronger. In mid-January 1919, the doctor stopped by and the news wasn't good.

The most the doctor could do was give Mary drugs, such as morphine or opium to control the pain. Her condition declined as February faded away.

It was in those last few days of February 1919, as Mary lingered somewhere between life and death, an intense storm began to build in the west. When it reached the northern coast of Lake Michigan, it had become one of northern Michigan's worst blizzards.

Gale force winds exceeding 60 miles an hour lashed the shores of Seul Choix Point and ravaged the lighthouse. Wind twisted the trees as if wheat in a field, slamming against the walls of the home. Like an invading army the wind and snow smashed the windows and assaulted the rooms.

It must have been terrifying for the children as William and Amanda rushed to board-up the windows against the freezing onslaught of snow. In the midst of all this lay Mary Pemble. What horror must have been going through her confused mind? Drugs and pain mingled with the sound of frightened children, shattering glass and the sudden, hard bite of cold. It must have seemed a living nightmare. Did she know what was happening or think she was in hell?

In time, the strength of the storm subsided, the winds calmed, and the life of Grandma Pemble was swept away.

After the storm travel was impossible for several days. The lighthouse was completely inaccessible. As a temporary measure, William Blanchard placed his mother-in-law in a section of the home where it was cold to preserve her remains. As Marilyn tells us, the area Mary was taken now contains the lighthouse and coast guard museum.

Kat and I wondered if the energies from any of these powerful events in the lighthouse's history had left an imprint. We hoped tonight's hunt would give us answers.

Before night settled, Kat and I wanted to check the top of the lighthouse. Tim and Brad didn't plan on investigating up there. They had never captured evidence in the tower, but really, how can you go to a lighthouse without climbing the tower. We ascended the narrow, winding, winding, winding... did we mention winding... stairway. Though not as tall as some of the lighthouses we have visited, the stairs seemed unusually steep and narrow. It was then we remembered our unused gym memberships and fear of heights.

At the top some UPPRS members were enjoying the incredible sunset over Lake Michigan. Kat and I smiled and nodded looking

Winding lighthouse stairs

relaxed and nonchalant hoping no one would notice our gasps for air. One of them turned and pointed. I looked in that direction and saw a small cluster of deer grazing in the grass. I wheezed at Kat, "Get some video of the deer."

Gripping the railing tightly with both hands, she wheezed back "No, I'm good here and I got em earlier as we were driving in." Apparently the bug-splattered window from her earlier video was no longer a problem.

Eventually we recovered and were able to appreciate the panoramic and peaceful scene before us. Dense woods opened to the wide expanse of Lake Michigan. The warm, amber glow of the sun spilled golden light over the water as it vanished beyond the horizon.

View at the top of the light tower

Turning around the cramped chamber of the tower, we quickly understood why Tim and Brad would not be investigating this area. The noise from the motor turning the still functional light was very loud, making EVP work out of the question. In addition, the staircase was so narrow and winding it would be impossible to position a video camera to cover more than a few feet.

Night was approaching and it was time to begin the investigation. UPPRS had their equipment positioned. They would be using video cameras and audio recorders strategically placed throughout the living quarters and basement. Members would carry thermo gages and EMF meters to check for sudden temperature variations or spikes in electromagnetic fields that may signal the beginning of paranormal activity.

The Upper Peninsula Paranormal Research Society members.
L to R: Tim, Lance. Michelle, Ryan, Matt and Brad.

This group also used Faraday cages for their audio recorders. A Faraday cage is a mesh container, made of a conducting material like metal or copper, into which the recorder is placed. Such an enclosure blocks out external static electric fields eliminating radio signal interference.

In the basement a fairly new piece of equipment was going to be tested. It was designed by UPPRS on the premise that spirits communicate by drawing energy from sources that generate electromagnetic fields. What they built was a mobile device, connected to its own power source that created a strong energy field. A video recorder was positioned near by in case a spirit did materialize.

Captain's kitchen frequently has place settings and chairs moving.

With everything ready to go, we went dark. My first tour of duty would be with Brad's team starting with a short stay in the captain's kitchen. I took a photo of the table to log placement of dishes and silverware. If one of the spirits should decide to play with the table setting, as they are known to do, we would know.

EVP questions were asked as we watched and waited. When nothing out of the ordinary happened we moved to the next location. Before leaving I placed an audio recorder on the table to record any possible anomalous sounds or voices that might occur later in the evening.

Our next stop was the basement. I followed the two men in the dark through a maze of small, cluttered rooms. Brick walls were stained and chipped with age. Each layer of peeling paint revealed another decade of the building's life.

We stopped in the section where Joseph Townshend's body was supposedly drained and embalmed. With a certain sense of foreboding, I scanned the sink and surrounding gloom. Dark streaks of rust stained the sink and gave the appearance of blood. I couldn't seem to look away. How appropriate that such a foul place would be used for this purpose.

Basement sink rumored to have a horrible past.

Brad began the EVP session. Our trio spent considerable time by the portable energy source hoping to draw out whatever spirits might remain.

Except for an eerie feeling, likely associated with the basement's dark and dingy atmosphere, this session was uneventful. The group continued its investigation on the outside grounds then moved back inside to the second floor bedrooms. Unfortunately, things were pretty uneventful for our team all night.

Meanwhile Kat was upstairs with Matt and Michelle from UPPRS. The two went into the captain's room while Kat stopped next door. Designed with a dark Victorian theme, this small room was filled with a collection of period pieces. The motionless form of a mannequin was standing beside the bed wearing a bonnet and dressed in a long black gown.

Turning, Kat stared into the mirror Marilyn believed was the home's portal to the other side.

She silently watched and waited, but the only thing that stared back was her own reflection and the frozen face of the mannequin.

Hearing Matt and Michelle begin their EVP session, she went to join them. The captain's room, like the other, was small and neat—not much space by today's standards. A small chest and bed filled the room. To the side, standing silent vigil was another mannequin dressed in an elegant wedding gown.

Matt tempted Joseph Townshend to come out with cigars he brought for the captain. When that didn't seem to work, Michelle took her turn. She spoke of her Ojibwa heritage. It was then she felt a change in temperature. Kat's thermo gage showed an increase going from 64 to 68.

As Michelle continued to talk about the Ojibwa people, the temperature rose to 72 and stayed there for a moment before dropping to 64. What was interesting is that the room's temperature remained steady. It was only the area around Michelle that fluctuated. Since she wasn't sitting near a vent or window the cause of the change was curious.

It was during our break sometime after midnight when a few members of UPPRS and myself heard music, almost like a trumpet. It was emanating from the rooms just off the kitchen. This was a newer section of the lighthouse where the assistant keepers and families used to stay. After a thorough examination, the source of the sound could not be found.

Some time later, Kat was drawn to the back to the museum. It was the room Marilyn had pointed out earlier as the area Mary "Grandma" Pemble's body had been placed. There seemed to be a slightly different atmosphere here than in the other rooms.

Feeling a sense of anticipation, Kat placed her audio recorder on a table and began a short series of questions, pausing after each. "We'd like to hear from you please. Just tell us your name. How old are you? What happened to you while you were here?"

After a brief period of time she turned and left. The recorder continued to run. Kat came downstairs and joined the others for a much needed break.

When the break was over, Kat followed Brad and Ryan to the upstairs bedroom believed to be the children's room. Earlier in the evening, when I was there with Brad, he had placed a toy wooden rocking horse on an old sewing machine table and positioned a video camera to record any movements.

Museum room where Grandma Pemble's body is
believed to have been placed after her death.

Brad began encouraging any child spirit to move the rocking
horse. His final remarks, "Let us know if there is any type of sign
you can give us, something unmistakable? If you can show yourself
to us or one of our camera setups, make this little horse move,
speak to us. We'd like to see you."

All eyes remained fixed on the little rocking horse. EMF
and temperature readings remained steady. With everything
unchanged and no unusual sounds being heard, Brad decided to
end the session.

The night's investigation was over. It ran seamlessly thanks to
the organized and efficient Upper Peninsula Paranormal Research
Society. Working with Tim, Brad and their group of experienced
investigators was a pleasure. They are a professional and committed
team looking for the paranormal truth. We look forward to working
with them in the future.

Kat and I left with a certain sense of disappointment. If
Captain Townshend or other resident lighthouse spirits remained
they were elusive this evening.

Through the years we have been on well over 100 investigations, and of those only a handful produced evidence. We would have to wait until all the material was reviewed to see if anything turned up. This was something UPPRS, Kat and I would be doing over the next several weeks.

It was our audio/video review ritual. We came in Monday morning not speaking to each other. Listening and watching hours of audio and video can be boring. Some days it puts us in a bad mood. That Monday morning was one of those "some days." We have learned there are times when not saying anything to each other is better.

By late afternoon we finished going over video and found one possible audio anomaly. It occurred when Kat was in the children's room with Brad and Ryan. Just as they were leaving, the audio on her camera seemed to pick up the soft words, "Come back." It was faint, but clarity was improved with a little audio adjustment. Some believe this is an actual EVP while others think it may be just an anomalous sound. It is on our Web site to review.

Evening approached and we were tired. With a full schedule for the next few days, further review would have to wait until the following week.

Later in the week Tim emailed a couple of suspect audio clips that were recorded upstairs while he was running and EVP session. It's believed the soft feminine voice said, "Here's captain." Upon review we all agreed it was likely voices from other team members. The voice on the second clip could not be understood. Tim suggested it might be Native American.

That motivated us to continue reviewing audio. Starting fresh the following Monday, maintaining our ritual of silence, the earphones went on and we began to pick up slight murmurs. Initially, the disembodied voices were such a low decibel they were almost imperceptible.

Most were residual, an imprint energy of a past event. One such example was captured in the hallway outside the assistant keepers' kitchen.

"Get out Hanson."

Did the spirit of Keeper Blanchard speak those words as he directed his assistant, William Hanson? Hanson served under Blanchard for many years before taking over the role of lighthouse keeper in 1942.

During the night's investigation, a recorder was left in the basement. Several EVPs were captured. One residual voice refers to nothing in particular. Brad and a member of his team were checking the portable energy source when this comes across, "You hate someone."

Another EVP responds to a question Brad asked. "Marilyn spends a lot of time here… is there anyone here that's attached to her… that might be sticking around here to see her?" The sharp, quick reply, "No."

Additional voices captured include, "Look at me, Diamo" and "Get out of the snow." Whether Diamo is a person's name or just a word is unclear. No one with that name could be associated with the lighthouse. Other disembodied voices can be heard in our Web site's Secret Room.

The next series of audio was a bit surprising. It occurred at the time Kat went to the coastguard museum and asked a few questions. It would appear that someone was attempting to reach out to Kat. Initially the words were overlooked. Some of the words are unclear but definitely a voice attempting to communicate.

Here is our interpretation.

Kat asks, "Just let us know your name."

Response: "Mary."

"How old are you?" The response was unclear.

Next question, "What happened to you while you were here?"

Response: "Died in snow."

Other words followed, but their interpretation remains elusive. Then just moments after Kat left the room came a loud, clear, almost desperate, "No." It's as if whoever remained wanted to be heard, wanted someone to know they were still there.

What stands out is the first direct response, "Mary." Our thoughts were immediately drawn to Mary Pemble who died during the snowstorm.

When Kat asked what happened to the spirit, the reply, "Died in snow." Certainly that would be an accurate description of Mary's death. It's particularly significant because when the storm blew in the windows, the interior of the house literally filled with snow. Even though Grandma Pemble wasn't actually outside in the snow, she obviously died in the midst of a major storm.

Another EVP was captured after Kat left to joined the others in the work area. Tim had been playing a collection of songs to try and attract the spirits, including The Edmund Fitzgerald and classics from the early 1900s.

The group was teasing him because he had such old-fashioned music stored in his computer's music library. To prove he was a hip man of the 21st century, Tim began to blast out Paralyzer by Finger Eleven. He cranked up the speakers to maximum volume. We all enjoyed Tim's coolness and his music. It seemed, however, that at least one unseen spirit disagreed. In the dark room away from our group, the recorder picked up a disembodied voice, "Too …too loud," or, "Too… too High." Apparently someone didn't appreciate Finger Eleven.

It was around 1:00 a.m. when Kat removed the recorder from that back room. Leaving, she gave a verbal time stamp to the audio misreading the time, saying it was ten minutes after two.

Fortunately the spirit in this room was intelligent and corrected Kat. The words, "No. One," were recorded.

For years Kat and I have wondered if Seul Choix Point Lighthouse is really haunted. Since the 1960s there has been much publicity surrounding the ghostly folklore and personal experiences encountered by many. Before our investigation we had never seen or heard valid evidence to support its wonderful ghost stories. In the back of our minds, we always suspected the stories were simply a way to draw tourists.

We have changed our minds, even though we didn't see the captain or catch a whiff of his cigar smoke. What we did find was the possibility that several different spirits may remain. The EVP evidence would indicate both residual and intelligent paranormal activity. It is possible Captain Joseph Willie Townshend is one of them.

However, what makes us want to return is what happened in the coast guard museum. It appears someone is anxiously trying to reach out and communicate, someone with the first name of Mary. We wonder if Mary Pemble isn't asking for help to find peace. Perhaps she remains confused, uncertain of what happened that fateful, stormy night. If it is Mary Pemble's spirit that remains in the quiet back room what she needs or wants remains unknown. Perhaps one day she'll find her way to the other side.

Story Five
Cobblestone Farms

2781 Packard Road, Ann Arbor, MI
Password: tic4044
Investigative Team:
Highland Ghost Hunters

Ann Arbor, home to the University of Michigan (Go Blue!). Its quaint downtown district is a hub of activity. People of all age groups and walks of life meander through its streets lined with an eclectic blend of boutique shops, independent book and music stores, coffeehouses, pubs, and elegant restaurants.

Though it has a small-town feel, Ann Arbor is actually a sophisticated community known for its state of the art technology, education and medicine. Much of its popularity has to do with an abundance of cultural offerings that appeal to many. From nationally acclaimed art festivals to museums and nightclubs, the city offers appealing activities for every visitor and resident.

Ann Arbor embraces its history. Just outside of the city limits, in Pittsfield Township, lies one of its hidden historical gems, Cobblestone Farm.

Built in the 1830s, it is nearly as old as the City of Ann Arbor. About thirty years ago, Ann Arbor purchased the farm and, with the help of the Cobblestone Farm Association, ensures ongoing restoration and maintenance. Today, on its beautifully maintained grounds, the association hosts seasonal programs, weddings and other celebratory events. Families often come to spend the day.

Though Cobblestone Farm is enjoyed by many, there are still countless others who drive by the quaint stone farmhouse on Packard Road oblivious of its past. And, for those who do come, how many stop to think that within the walls of this historic home are the memories of the Ticknor, Booth and Campbell families. Real people, real families and a home filled with their love, laughter, sadness and tragedies.

How strong are the energies of these families and is it possible their spirits remain? For some time there have been reports of unusual phenomena at the home. The vision of a woman was seen looking out from an upper floor window. Other reports include the apparition of a man seated in the dining room and another of a little boy who supposedly drowned in the well on the home's property. We hoped to find out if any of these reports were true during our investigation.

It was a beautiful but cool spring evening. We met Jenny Marcus and Lisa Mann, founders of Highland Ghost Hunters, at a local eatery before heading out to Cobblestone Farm. Joining them on this hunt were teammates, Scott and Sue.

Over dinner, the evening's strategy was discussed. Of course, there was still plenty of time to share other important topics of the day. This led to Jenny telling us about her culinary expertise and how frozen tacos can just explode in a microwave oven for no apparent reason.

After a few laughs and a good dinner, we headed over to Cobblestone Farm. Waiting for us were several welcoming members of the Cobblestone Farm Association, including George Taylor, President; Jane Carr, Vice President; Tracey Miller, Secretary; and Jane's brother, Ray. After introductions they took us on a tour of the property and shared some of its history.

Cobblestone Farm Association L to R:
George Taylor, President; Jane Carr, Vice President; Tracey Miller, Secretary.

Dr. Benajah Ticknor was a well-respected surgeon with the United States Navy. As he neared retirement, he began looking for places to settle down. Benajah eventually chose Michigan because of its affordable land costs.

In 1835, Benajah asked his brother, Heman, to help scout out good land. Since Heman was also interested in relocating to Michigan, he was happy to assist. He found a small cabin on 183 acres of farmland in Pittsfield and purchased it from Ezra Maynard on behalf of his brother. Shortly after, Heman, his wife and their six children moved into the cabin and began farming the land.

During those first years, Benajah and his wife, Getia, were seldom around. Most of the doctor's time was spent at sea or on duty in naval hospitals on the East Coast.

It wasn't until a visit in 1840 that Benajah noticed how cramped the family's quarters were and decided a larger home was in order. Construction of the cobblestone house began soon thereafter and was eventually completed in 1844. This was the beginning of Cobblestone Farm's incredible history.

Benajah Ticknor

Courtesy Cobblestone Farm Association

The life of a farming family, especially in those early days, was difficult. Long hours and hard work were a part of that life and so was death. Sadly, Heman Ticknor and his wife, Eliza, lost 11 of their 12 beloved children. Five of them died at the farmhouse. Their deaths were not merciful, quick, or painless. An inflammation of the brain took one, Tuberculosis three, and typhoid fever another.

A sick room was setup on the first floor to care for the children. Initially, each feared their disease and impending death, but when their time came they were ready to meet God. As the obituary of their daughter, Caroline, reads:

"Her last hours were peaceful and her death tranquil. Conscious that end was near, she called for her physician and asked how many minutes she had to live. 'Not long' was the response. Hers was the only dry eye. Hers the only calm voice, as with more natural composure, she said, 'Weep not for me,' as she bade each friend adieu."

In grief, the family's bond grew closer.

Benajah met his own demise in 1858. Two years later, his widow sold a portion of the land to Heman and the remainder to the Horace Booth family.

Under the Booth family, the farm prospered. Horace's son, Nelson Booth, raised and sold nursery stock and expanded the Ticknor apple orchard. He was also a fancier of thoroughbred racing horses and found considerable success in their racing and breeding.

In 1880 the Booths sold the property. It changed hands twice before being purchased by William Campbell. The farm remained with the Campbells from 1881 to the 1970s.

They were a very close-knit family. Though serious about work, they shared a great sense of humor, quick with a smile and a lighthearted joke. William's son, Robert, enjoyed the new and novel hobby of photography and captured many of the family's good times on film. Their closeness was obvious.

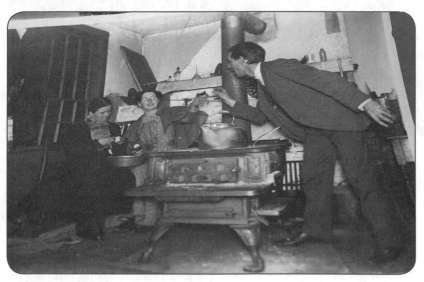

The Campbell family loved having fun and the new hobby of photography.

The farm prospered as a result of the Campbell's innovate farming approach and prized herds of Durham cattle and sheep. Life was good as the decades rolled by; then came the 1920s. Though much of America prospered, it was tough economic times for farmers. The Campbells were struggling but managed to hold on until the fire of 1924.

Mary Campbell, a child at the time of the fire, recalled the events of that tragic day. It was around sunset. Mary was in the kitchen looking out the window and noticed a beautiful reddish glow reflecting on the buildings. Thinking it was the setting sun she called her mother to see. When her mother got there, she immediately knew it wasn't the sun. The barn was burning.

The kitchen looks very much like it did in its early days.

In those days, a barn was the heart of a farm. Everything was kept there, including supplies, expensive vehicles and machinery.

Intense flames spiraled into the air and could be seen for quite a distance. Hot embers drifted to outlying buildings and within a short time nearly all the farm's buildings were aflame. In a desperate attempt to save their home, the Campbell's threw wet comforters and blankets on the roof. Water supplies ran out as their cisterns dried up or were consumed in flames.

When the smoke settled, the house was saved but just about everything else was destroyed. The Campbell's were devastated and never fully recovered from this terrible loss.

How the fire began remains a mystery. Some speculated Mary's brother, William, might have been the incendiary. His actions were sometimes unpredictable and erratic. Even an uncle was a suspect.

However, something happened just days before the mysterious blaze which might also explain its cause. Henry Ford had visited the farm in search of antique equipment for his new venture, The Henry Ford Museum and Greenfield Village. He found an old reaper in the Campbell's barn and made plans to have it picked up for his collection. Unfortunately the reaper was destroyed in the fire.

During an interview, Mary made a comment that added to the mystery. Apparently, there had been barn fires at other locations following Mr. Ford's visits.

At this time in American history, Henry Ford was a controversial figure because of his outspoken social and political views as well as anti-union activities. He was not well loved by all. Could the fire have been started by one of Mr. Ford's strong adversaries? Perhaps it was someone who wanted to destroy his dream by preventing construction of The Henry Ford Museum.

After the fire, the Campbells began to slowly sell off parcels of land to pay the bills. Mary and her brother, George, remained in the home until the death of their brother, William. He died of a heart attack in the early 1970s somewhere on the grounds of Cobblestone Farm.

With our tour completed and points of paranormal activity identified, it was time to begin the investigation. There was a lot of ground to cover and Highland Ghost Hunters wasted no time setting up equipment.

The first floor gift shop that had served as

(L) Lisa Mann and (R) Jenny Marcus getting ready

the Ticknor family sick room would be covered. Cameras were also positioned in the attic, dining room, bedrooms and staircase. These areas had reports of apparitions, voices and footsteps.

(L) Sue and (R) Scott take equipment setup seriously.

Yet another place of interest was the Willis Log Cabin, built around 1837. It was moved from Willis, Michigan, to the Cobblestone property in 1981. Though there had been no reports of paranormal activity here, because of its age, Jenny and Lisa thought it might carry some type of spirit energy.

Additional time would be spent in the barn. Jane mentioned several members had heard frequent and unusually loud bangs. Some so loud they were almost threatening in volume.

The new barn built on the same site as the original out buildings.

We wondered why such a new building, constructed in the 1980s, might be paranormally active. Then Jane informed us it sat on the foundations of the original out buildings destroyed in the 1924 fire. There may be some relationship to the activity and the events surrounding that fire.

Once equipment was set, Jenny and Lisa broke the team in groups and the investigation began. All was quiet until Lisa's team and Bev, entered the attic. A narrow stairway led them to the gloomy confines of the uppermost floor. Moonlight spilled across the cluttered room revealing countless heirlooms.

The small group carefully made their way to the center of the room and sat down. Almost instantly faint sounds crept from the darkest corners. Initially they were ignored, the team thinking it was just the sounds of an old home. Yet, there was a prevailing sense that something was near.

Sue, a member of the Highland team, began the questioning. "Is there anybody in the attic? Do you want to come and talk to us here?"

Silence. Then, ever so subtle, the quiet in the room was interrupted by indefinable sounds, a collection of hushed whispers, creaks or groans.

Lisa wondered if it might be something else. "Is someone trying to communicate with us?" Nothing but dead air and the sounds of their shallow breathing.

The questions continued and for the most part centered on the children. Then a voice, soft and low that only Lisa heard. It was an unusual sound, perhaps a word tinged with a foreign dialect or accent. She wasn't certain.

The attic where Lisa thought she heard a voice.

Sometime later, the sounds in the attic quieted. It seemed whatever had been there was gone. Everyone headed downstairs to their next location.

Meanwhile, I was in the first floor sick room with Jane, Tracey, George and Scott. I called out to Abigail or Caroline, coaxing them to come near the device with the green light on it (the EMF meter). There were no movements or sounds throughout our time here, at least none that we noticed.

The gift shop was used as a sick room for the Ticknor family.

The next several hours our teams traveled between locations. The investigation moved smoothly but from our prospective, unremarkably.

After a break Jenny's team, along with Ray, George and Bev headed to the Willis Log Cabin while Lisa, Scott, Jane, Tracey and I went to the barn. It had been a tiring investigation and we were getting a little crazy.

To be honest, though loud knocks had been heard in the barn, we weren't expecting much to happen. Even in total darkness, this place was very comfortable and the atmosphere pleasant.

Everyone was a little lighthearted and a bit silly as chairs were positioned in a circle near the center of the room. As we sat, Tracey skillfully recreated the memorable scene from the Blair Witch movie. She brought my camera close to her face, and muttered, "I'm so scared." We all chuckled. It was an Academy Award winning performance.

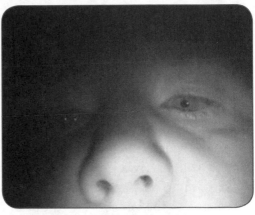

Tracey Miller's acting début.

Eventually our group settled down and Lisa began the EVP session. "Is there anyone here that would like to communicate with us?"

The EMF meter was flat. In the silence, smiles were exchanged. No one expected a response. That's when the first light knock was heard. It was likely just the wood barn's natural sounds.

Lisa continued, "We mean you no harm." Her eyes scanned the darkness of the empty room.

She turned to Jane, "You said it was built in the 1980s."

"Yes, but it was built on the site…" Her words were interrupted when another soft knock was heard. Jane was about to remind us it had been built on the exact site of the original barn.

Again, everyone dismissed the sounds as natural settling. Then the third knock came. Smiling, I threw out the possibility that it could be a spirit responding and suggested the questions continue.

Scott took the suggestion. "If that was you, could you do that again for us? Let us know you're here so we know that's not just a coincidence."

Another rap came from somewhere in the barn, but this time much louder. "Okay," Scott's voice trailed off as his eyes searched the darkness.

"That was pretty loud." I murmured.

He agreed and continued. "Not to push my luck with you but...." His words cut off by a sharp bang, even louder than the last.

With raised eyebrows, we all shared a common question, was it indeed a response? Lisa checked EMF levels and temperature. Both remained steady.

None of us were ready to claim the sound paranormal, though we did wonder at its cause. Wind was dismissed. The night was very still, barely a breeze. The only other natural explanation was expanding and contracting wood. Yet, the steadily increasing volume to the bangs seemed out of the ordinary.

I took a turn. "If that's someone trying to talk to us, that's fantastic. Do you mind us being here? If you could make that noise once for yes, twice for no."

We listened as one light tap was followed by a second. Surprise filled Jane's eyes as she glanced at Tracey.

For a brief moment, all was quiet then a resounding boom that literally shook the walls. That got our attention.

Lisa directed her flashlight to the EMF meter and saw levels were beginning to rise. It signaled an increase in energy that is said to build when a spirit nears. Scott, taking Lisa's digital thermal gage, went up to the balcony hoping its higher elevation would help him pinpoint the location of the sound, should it come again. He aimed the thermometer's laser beam near Lisa and our circle. It was a steady 73 degrees.

I began a new series of questions about the fire. "Whoever is here, did you start the fire that burned these buildings down? Are you afraid to show yourself? Do you not want to get caught?"

Barn's upper balcony

Tracey added, "Was it an accident?"

It was then Lisa felt a tingling sensation as the hair on her left arm began to rise. It lasted briefly then faded just as Tracey felt a chill. The energy in the room was building.

It seemed the last series of questions might have stirred something up, so I continued.

"Did you set this fire? Are you the one that burned this building down? Why did you do it? Are you a coward? Tell us what you did."

Tracey feels a chill.

Scott's voice echoed down from the balcony. Temperature had risen from 73 to 81 degrees.

"Was it an accident?" I continued.

Scott's words again carried down to us, "Woah, woah, woah!" The air around him had gotten very thick and he felt the hair rise on his neck. Lisa noted EMF levels had edged upward from .5 to .9.

EMF Spike

I began a more aggressive series of questions telling whatever remained that it was time to stop hiding, stop being a coward to come out and confess. EMF levels elevated with each use of the word, "coward" and then began to bounce erratically until it shot up to 2.1. I stopped speaking and watched as levels returned to normal.

Kat's questions
become more aggressive.

Glances were exchanged among our group. This was getting interesting.

Lisa gently said, "You don't have to hide anymore."

I continued, "If we can help you, we will try to do that. But we can't do anything unless you want to talk to us. Come out."

Lisa began to feel that tingling sensation again. It was strange. She didn't really feel cold yet her left arm had goose bumps and every hair stood on end.

Lisa experiences a tingling sensation on her arms.

I placed my hand near her arm and felt a definite coolness then glanced down at the meter. It had rocketed to 4.6. Scott called down, the temperature was up to 87 degrees. Now that was crazy!

Lisa and I shared a quick glance. This significant increase in both EMF and temperature

EMF reached 4.9 with a temperature of 91 degrees before things settled down.

levels could indicate a paranormal event was beginning. The sudden rise in temperature was curious. The general theory is that temperatures drop when a spirit enters a room. This is believed to be a result of the spirit drawing energy to itself. It pulls that energy from many sources, including heat from the air, which drops the temperature. In this case, however, the temperature was rising.

We sat in unnerving silence. Waiting. My mind drifted again to the terrible fire. It started in the old barn and traveled to the out buildings on which this new barn was built. Could these rising temperatures be associated with the fire?

Though a disaster for the Campbell family, no deaths were reported, at least no one known. The blaze had been intense, its flames an inferno, and the amount of charred debris in its aftermath massive. Was it possible someone died in the fire and their remains overlooked?

I began directing questions along those lines. As I did, the temperature began to increase, slowly rising from 73 to over 91 degrees.

Lisa and Tracey stood and left the circle, briefly overwhelmed by the intensity of feelings they were experiencing. Taking one or two steps back they immediately noted a change in atmosphere. They stated it was much calmer outside of the circle.

The circle's dissolving marked the culmination of whatever had occurred. Temperatures and EMF levels returned to normal and the heaviness vanished.

What just happened?

Checking our watches, we were surprised to discover more than an hour passed. It had seemed like minutes.

Sounds were heard outside. It was the other team arriving from their investigation of the Willis Log Cabin. The side door opened and Jenny peaked through with Bev and the others close behind. According to Jenny, the log cabin had been pretty quiet.

Standing L-R: George, Kat, Jane, Susie, Jenny, Lisa, Scott
Seated L-R: Bev, Tracey, Ray

We shared the strange events in the barn with everyone. Jenny, Lisa and Sue vowed to return, which they did 20 minutes later. It was quiet for the first few minutes until Lisa's questions began.

"Did you get mad at Kat when she called you a coward?" A distant rap was heard.

"If that was you could you do it again? Kat called you a coward. She told you that you were afraid."

Jenny asked, "Did that upset you. Did is upset you when she was talking to you like that?"

Lisa, "You can answer our questions by knocking one time for yes and two times for no."

Jenny asked again, "Did that bother you when she spoke that way?"

Seconds ticked by, then it came, one thunderous bang. They jumped as the sound reverberated through the empty room.

"Oh my, God." Sue whispered.

Lisa confirmed, "That's what we were hearing."

Jenny was incredulous. "That just scared the holy heck out of me!"

During the next 30 or 40 minutes, questions continued. The knocks became less frequent and finally subsided. As their time in the barn concluded, Jenny, Lisa and Sue reluctantly left hoping audio or video would reveal evidence that the knocks were a response to their questions.

In the early hours of the morning we called it a wrap. Saying our goodbyes to George, Jane, Tracey and Ray and thanking them for bravely sticking it out with us to the bitter end, we headed home.

A week later we received a call from Jenny and Lisa. Though nothing had turned up on video, they had captured some interesting EVPs. After listening to them, Bev and I got excited. We cleared off our schedules for the day and began our own review of what we had recorded.

All of us were shocked at the volume of evidence collected. The first series of EVPs were recorded within the first minute of Lisa's team settling in the attic.

It began when Sue turned to Ray and said, "I'm sorry, I can't remember your name."

Ray responded. What no one heard, however, was the other response. The whispered, "Winona." Seconds after that, "Go back."

Sue continued, "Is there anybody in the attic?" We are not certain of the exact words. It's very quiet and may say "I hear you" or a long extended "yessss."

The last in this series came with Sue's next question. "Does anyone want to come and talk to us here?" The soft reply, "No."

At the time Lisa thought she heard a soft voice with an accent, these whispered words were heard, "Here I am." The words did, in fact, have an accident. The last word "am" sounded more like *yeem*.

As far as the name, Winona, we found several first names but we were unable to find anyone with that last name in the Ann Arbor area. Should we discover something after the publishing of this book, we will post it in our Web site's Secret Room.

Other interesting EVPs came in the master bedroom. This bedroom is believed to be Benajah Ticknor and his wife's. While Lisa's group was in the attic and our group was downstairs, a single word was recorded, "Ben."

Next came audio from my time in the sick room. We were standing just outside when the first EVP occurred. It is believed to say, "Jay Ticknor." There are a few interpretations of the first name. One is "Jane" the other "Shane" but the last name of Ticknor seems fairly certain.

There was an Ellen *Jane* Ticknor in the family. She was Heman's daughter and born at Cobblestone Farm. Ellen *Jane* was very ill with consumption (TB) but actually passed away in a home across the street in 1864. It could also be that Benajah Ticknor had the nickname of Jay (Bena-*jah*).

A few minutes into our sick room EVP session the name "Buck Weiner" was captured. From the diary of Robert C. Campbell, we know the Campbells sold oats and other goods to the Weiner family.

The unusual events that transpired in the barn did provide some surprising audio. The threatening sound of bangs quieted about 30 minutes into the investigation. It was after that we began picking up EVPs on the recorder. Some were so quiet we had to discard them for this story. Here are some of the more significant EVPs captured.

The first occurred about 55 minutes into the audio, while investigating the barn. I was asking some aggressive questions frequently using the word "coward." A whispered voice replied, "Hate you."

"It's on fire here," was recorded just seconds before Scott informed us the temperature had risen to 90.

At one point I asked if someone died in the barn fire, then added, "We need to find you." A hushed response says, "Find me."

There were other EVPs collected when Jenny, Lisa and Sue returned to the barn late in the investigation. The first was heard as Lisa was telling Sue about her earlier experience in the barn. She was describing how she felt when an unknown voice says, "Pull it together."

The evening's investigation held more surprises than we could have anticipated. Of course, we're still not ready to say the loud bangs in the barn were ghosts. Yet, the EVPs collected in both the home and barn lead us to believe there is something paranormal going on at Cobblestone Farm.

What continues to baffle us is the mystery surrounding the fire that consumed the Campbell's barn. Is there someone trying to reach out from the other side, eager to finally let the truth be known?

Whatever remains at Cobblestone Farm, one thing is certain; this home on Packard Road will remain forever a part of the Ticknor, Booth and Campbell families. Where once it was the families that brought the home life, it is the now the home that brings them life. This is certainly part of what makes Cobblestone Farm such a remarkable and cherished place in Ann Arbor, Michigan.

Story Six
Perry's Grand
Arlington Hotel

201 South Linn St., Bay City, MI
Password: mmm201
Investigative Team:
Mid Michigan Paranormal Investigators

There was something different about Perry's Grand Arlington Hotel as we approached from South Linn Street, not because of the size. It isn't a particularly large building. It wasn't because of the architecture, which is traditional nineteenth century. It was simply a sense that there was more to this former hotel, now pub, than its understated appearance revealed.

My eyes were drawn to the third floor and one particular window. It was boarded up. Perhaps that's what brought it to my attention. Or it might have been my thoughts of Emory Fritz. Emory was just 42 years old when he jumped to his death from a third floor room on a hot August day in 1910.

I turned to Bev, "Interesting place."

"It is." She replied, her eyes scanning the upper floor. "I wonder if anyone still lives up there."

"Why? Do the boarded windows remind you of home?"

She gave me *that look*, "Ha-ha, very funny. Actually, it looks more like my car that we seem to *always* use on these trips. By the way, I believe you left your dirty laundry in the back seat from the last one."

"Oh! I wondered what happened to my blue sweater."

We walked down the street in silence giving us the opportunity to check out the downtown district of West Bay City. It's like a walk through time. Brick front stores, many of which date back to the 1800s and early 1900s, line the main streets.

The Arlington Hotel is located in West Bay City that, as the name implies, sits on the west bank of the Saginaw River. Back in 1865, the west side was called Wenona, named for the mother in Longfellow's poem "Hiawatha." With the town's rapid growth, in 1877 the name changed to West Bay City.

Today the town is an interesting blend of gift and antiques shops, restaurants and a variety of pubs. In fact, the number of pubs in West Bay City make it quite a party town on the weekends. At this particular time of the day, however, the streets were quiet and the Arlington Hotel waited.

It was originally built 1867 by the Bunnel brothers as a wood-frame hotel known as the Bunnel House. Unfortunately, within the first year, a massive fire took it down. In 1868 it was rebuilt using brick. Louis Potter purchased the hotel in 1882, then named the Wells House, and renamed it the Arlington Hotel. The name and ownership has changed several times in the hotel's more than 140 years eventually returning to its earlier name of Arlington Hotel.

Arlington Hotel at the turn of the century.

Courtesy of the Arlington Hotel

As mentioned, though the word "hotel" remains in Arlington's name, it is primarily a bar. Though a few rooms on the second floor are available for rent, the majority remain vacant. The third floor is a deteriorated shell of vacant rooms and, as we would soon discover, uninhabitable.

Bev and I stepped through the front door of the Arlington entering into a large room that once served as the main lobby. Dark paneled walls and high ceilings were a clear reminder of its 1800's construction. Those were the days of grand entrances and a reminder that, at one point in time, the Arlington Hotel was one of West Bay City's finest lodgings.

Just ahead was a stairway to the upper floors. Left was the entrance to a narrow barroom. The bar's overall appearance could best be described as old-time hip. Its décor is very much like it might have been in the early 1900s. The turn-of-the-century look is offset by a few modern features, like the long shuffleboard table resting along one wall and an assortment of hanging promotional banners highlighting the latest brews.

To the right of the main lobby is another open area, once the hotel's dining room. It is now the bar's game room with a couple of pool tables setup and ready for play.

Matt and Melanie Moyer, founders of Michigan Paranormal Investigators were heading this case. They were already huddling with their team members organizing equipment for tonight's investigation.

Matt Moyer (L), Co-founder of Mid Michigan Paranormal Investigators, discussing the evenings equipment setup with team member, John (R).

As always, it was great to see them. Over the past couple of years, Bev and I have gotten to know Matt, Melanie and their team members pretty well. Experienced and dedicated investigators, they know what they're doing and have become our good friends.

Melanie broke away from the team to introduce us to the saloon's current manager who shared some of the hotel's ghostly stories. We began in the bar where, during odd hours, the apparitions of children were seen. He also told us the faucets behind the bar turned on for no apparent reason. As explained, he would arrive in the morning to find the faucets on full blast, even though he had made sure they were completely off the previous night.

Next was the ladies room, just behind the main floor stairway. There have been several reports of women hearing disembodied voices or the sound of someone in the room though they were completely alone. The manager informed us this hadn't always been the ladies room. No one was certain exactly what its original purpose had been.

Reentering the lobby the manager pointed to the staircase. He informed us that, in the old days, the stairs had been much wider and open all the way to the third floor. There had been stories that a bartender had died either throwing himself off or accidently falling from the third floor hallway all the way down to the lobby.

With that he led us up the stairway. The old, wooden steps groaned and creaked under our feet and echoed off the walls as we made our way past the second floor to the third. There had never been reports of paranormal activity on the second floor. It all seemed to center on the third.

The long, third floor hallway seemed to stretch on forever. Gouged and crumbling walls and ceilings exposed the building's skeleton beneath. Our feet crunched over paint chips and other scattered debris as we made our way to the floor's single bathroom. It was a long, narrow room with layers of dirt and rust staining the claw-foot tub. The small sink wasn't any better. Obviously, the bathroom along with the other rooms hadn't been used in decades.

Third floor is reported to be very active.

There are tales that a woman was murdered in this bathtub. As the story goes, a prostitute or girlfriend was discovered by her lover in a romantic relationship with another man. In a jealous rage, he entered the bathroom and shot her.

A dark, ghostly apparition has been seen wandering the hall. Though it isn't certain if the shadow is that of a man or a woman, most seem to believe it is the spirit of the woman who was killed.

The manager took us to the room where this woman was supposed to have stayed. It was small and dreary with aged floral wallpaper and the mustiness of many years. A portion of the ceiling was gone, its remnants scattered on the floor around us. This was a room we would have to investigate later.

Melanie and the manager continued down the hallway as Bev and I headed in the opposite direction to the back room with the boarded window. This is the area that initially caught our attention earlier. We stood silently for several minutes taking in the small quarters. It looked much like the other chambers, though the walls seemed to have considerably more graffiti.

Did a man jump to his death from this boarded-up window?

Standing quietly, there was a certain sense of anticipation. Bev and I have no level of sensitivity. It's not like we usually walk into a room and automatically *know* if there is a spirit present. I'm not exactly sure what the two of us were expecting but whatever it was eluded us.

After a few minutes, we rejoined Melanie and the manager who were going to the basement. The four of us traveled precariously down the worn, uneven steps into the damp, musty, coldness below. Heavy wood beams were interspersed with stone and brickwork, revealing the hotel's original foundations. Lights cast deep shadows in the farthest corners and reflected off the fine tendrils of spider webs giving them an almost ethereal luminescence.

I stepped on a piece of plywood lying on the floor disturbing an unnaturally large, black spider with thick, hairy legs. This creature fearlessly stood its ground almost daring us to do something, then rapidly skidded into a dark crevice of the wall. I jumped over the remaining wood plank. Good grief, I hate spiders!

Our small group eventually settled into a section to the left of the stairs. It was explained that, in its earlier days, there was a sunken sidewalk in front of the hotel. The basement once contained the hotel's poolroom and barbershop, along with other small businesses.

As our eyes began to focus on the gloomy interior, the vision of collapsed windows and doorways, now filled with rocks and cement, began to take shape. Window and door frames, now crumpled, were made from fine wood. Moving from room to room was like walking through an underground ghost town revealing a graveyard of past lives. In one section, we noted remnants of wallpaper. It was a floral design, similar to some of the old guest rooms on the third floor. We wondered if someone had lived down here.

The gloomy basement may have a speakeasy past.

Our attention was diverted as the manager began talking about the reports of apparitions seen and heard in this region of the basement. Several employees refused to come down here by themselves.

With that, the tour was over. Before returning to the main floor, the manager paused for a moment to show us an old bar top leaning against the stairway. One of the stories associated with the hotel is that it served as a speakeasy during prohibition. The bar top was supposedly the one used during those days. It wasn't much to look at, but what it represented was interesting.

The days of prohibition were filled with bootleg liquor, gambling, violent criminal gangs, and police crackdowns. Though liquor was illegal, many popular restaurants and nightclubs had a *secret area* for their select guest to enjoy a drink and a game of cards. Special guests were asked to keep these rooms secret and not speak openly about their existence. Hence the term *speakeasy*.

This time in America also brought in a new breed of women. These ladies shunned moral norms. They bobbed their hair, wore scandalously short skirts, drank hard whiskey and otherwise flaunted their disdain for what was considered acceptable behavior for young women. They were known as the *flappers*.

Bev and I would have to look into the speakeasy rumor. This could add a new dimension to the Arlington's possible haunting.

Returning to the main floor, Matt and Melanie gathered everyone together and divided us into teams. Bev would be joining Melanie on the second floor while I would go with Matt to the basement.

Melanie, John, Aaron, Frank and Bev slowly made their way down the murky hallway, echoes of their footsteps followed. Two rooms had renters. Of the two residents only one, a woman, would be in the hotel for the night. The woman was told about the hunt and agreed to remain in her room for the evening.

Melanie and the others eventually settled into an open suite with a living area, kitchen and two-bedrooms. In earlier days, the second floor contained larger rooms for meetings or receptions. In later years, they were converted to apartments.

John and Aaron ran the thermal imaging camera and slowly scanned the room for anomalous heat variations. It's believed a spirit's form will be picked up on the thermal imager through a distinct temperature signature. Nothing unusual was detected for this sweep.

Melanie led the first EVP session, throwing out questions hoping for some type of response. It was just after 9:30 P.M. when a suspicious creaking sound was heard from the hallway that sounded very much like footsteps. Melanie picked up the flashlight and her camera and darted into the dark corridor. A gasp was heard as Melanie, unknowingly, directed the bright beam of her flashlight into the startled eyes of the boarder.

After a nervous little chuckle, the tenant softly murmured she was getting ready to take a shower before going to bed. Melanie's compassionate response was, "No, you're not! We're investigating. You can take your shower in an hour."

The young woman meekly nodded and, taking her big fluffy towel, went back to her room. Melanie is a very petite woman, but nobody messes with her. Coming back into the room, Melanie shook her head. She felt bad about what she had just done, but the sound from a shower would contaminate audio.

Their investigation of the second floor continued until excited voices were heard from two people stationed near the barroom. The team quickly returned to the first floor and entered the bar. The sink's faucet was running full blast. Melanie turned it off, closing the handle very tightly. It was possible the faucet had not been completely turned off. In most instances, a faucet unexpectedly turning on is more of a plumbing problem than a sign of ghostly activity. They remained in the bar and began a vigil to see if the faucet would turn on with provocation. It did not.

Melanie's team checks the bar
for possible activity.

Meanwhile, Matt, Jeff, Steve and I were in the basement conducting an EVP session. I was moving cautiously. My eyes kept darting to the place where that horrific, hairy-legged spider had made an appearance an hour ago. I knew he was hiding in there somewhere with his wife and their 500 babies. So far none of them had shown their ugly heads.

Forcing my attention back to Matt and the others, I watched and listened as they read off EMF levels. Electro magnetic fields were consistently high, which usually means its coming from an electrical source. In this case, wires in the ceiling and light fixtures were leaking EMF like crazy. High electro magnetic fields can affect a person's perception. This can cause some to feel uneasy, fearful and sometimes nauseous.

Matt continued to lead EVP sessions in different sections of the basement. The team was settled down in a back area when Matt came to attention. "I saw a shadow!" Jeff excitedly agreed.

Matt pointed in the direction of the basement where apparitions had been reported. We were there in an instant but nothing was found. Matt told us it swiftly darted toward the exit stairs.

We moved further into the basement, in the opposite direction of the exit. To our surprise, there was another stairway. It was rickety,

Matt leading an EVP
session in the basement.

and seemingly abandoned leading to an ancient door that was blocked off. Matt considered the possibility the stairway may have been used during prohibition. It certainly was old enough for that to be possible.

Matt began another series of EVP questions near the abandoned stairs. The questions resulted in dead air. If there was something down here, it was gone. Our time in the basement had ended and we went upstairs. Before leaving, I placed my audio recorder where the shadow had been seen then bid a fond adieu to the hairy-legged spider and his ugly family.

Our investigation continued in the bar and game room. Bev and Melanie's group headed to the third floor, their first stop the bathroom. It was here the woman had supposedly been killed by her jealous boyfriend or husband. Bev placed her audio recorder on the sink.

Stairs that led to nowhere.

Melanie got into the tub and began a series of questions focusing on the woman who was said to have died. While this was going on, John and Aaron continuously scanned the room and hallway with the thermal imager. To the team's frustration, nothing happened. After twenty minutes, even though Melanie seemed pretty darned comfortable in the tub, the others felt cramped. It was time to continue the investigation in other rooms.

EMF readings were taken and, just like the basement, were unusually high. Though the electricity was off on this floor and the old wires cut,

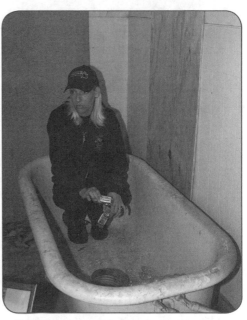

Melanie attempting to draw a response from the woman who was supposedly killed.

they were grounded. Grounded wires, no matter how old, still generate EMF.

The group made their way down the hall, finally stopping in the last room with the boarded window. John and Aaron entered with the thermal imager. Bev followed close behind, video camera in hand. Aaron scanned the room while John carefully watched the monitor for unusual heat variations.

Aaron abruptly stopped, angling the imager to the floor. He turned his head back to John and quietly said, "There's a fading handprint on the floor. Do you see it?"

"Yeah, I see that."

Bev and Melanie looked at the monitor and saw the fading heat signature of a five-finger handprint.

John reached down to check it out. "It's going away. It's fading away."

"Was it cold?" Melanie was referring to the heat signature recorded on the imager.

"No, it's warm. It was a handprint. It's almost gone now."

The third floor had been vacant for the last couple of hours. Certainly no one had been in the room since Melanie's group began their investigation 30 minutes earlier. Even then, if someone had come back and placed their hand on the floor it would have left an impression. The floor was covered with dust. Their footprints could easily be seen but the dust was undisturbed where the image of the hand appeared. It was completely untouched.

Melanie encouraged whoever was in the room to give them another sign. Bev asked if they would touch the wall or ceiling and leave another handprint.

With no noticeable response and no additional thermal hits, everyone moved outside into the hall. It was possible the spirit energy might have moved into other rooms. For the next 15 to 20 minutes they searched in vain. Nearing the end of their time, they decided to return once more to the back room with the boarded window.

John and Aaron were the first to enter with Bev close behind. Melanie had just entered when the men looked up at each other then turned to Bev.

"Did somebody just have their hand on the wall? Bev, did you have your hand on the wall?"

"No, I've got the camera in my hands."

John nodded his head and calmly replied, "There's a new hand print on the wall."

Bev positioned her video camera on the thermal imager. It was clear, another heat signature of a perfect, five-finger handprint. Everyone took turns positioning their hand near the print but none matched. Obviously, it had not come from any visible person in the room.

Aaron (L) and John (R)
examine rooms with the thermo imager.

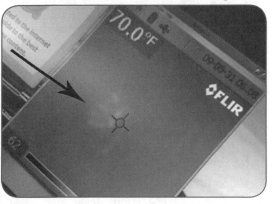
The five finger handprint
did not match anyone's hand in the room.

Everyone began encouraging the spirit to communicate. No response. All they could do was watch as the heat signature slowly faded away.

On their way downstairs, John shared his earlier experience. Setting up equipment on the third floor he had seen a black shadow run across the hall near the staircase. Of course, as is all too frequent, the apparition was not recorded. If it's not recorded, it didn't happen. That's the rule Mid Michigan, Bev and I always follow.

During a break, Melanie's team told us about the bizarre handprints the thermal imager had captured. We were excited. That was our next stop. After an uneventful time on the first floor, we were hoping for something a little more interesting than the sound of our own voices.

After the break, Melanie's team went to the basement while our group moved to the third floor. We immediately entered the now infamous back room where the handprints were seen.

Melanie had warned us that EMF levels in this room were very high. She was certainly right. They exceeded 8.0. A normal EMF reading is less than 1.0.

I began the questioning by asking if Emory Fritz, the man who committed suicide, was in the room. I asked why he left his wife and children.

Matt continued, "Was it a really bad time when there was no work?"

I asked if he was a coward for ending his life that way. Jeff, sitting in a corner with a sound sensitive headphone, heard a whispered voice after my statement. He thought it had said *no*.

Jeff took his turn, "Were you pushed out the window?"

"Wow, it feels like I have to cry." We turned to one of the members of our group to see tears running down his face. He wiped them away, overwhelmed with emotions and had to leave the room.

Matt continued, "Emory if you're here and really depressed and sad … we can't understand what's happening to you unless you communicate with us; and we want to help you even if it's just to talk to you."

After Matt's words, the previously high EMF levels began to dissipate moving from 5.2 to 3.4. Believing the energy may be leaving, Matt began a new series of questions hoping to pull it back.

"Did you feel like you let down somebody?" EMF went up to 4.2 then dropped to 4.1. It repeated this pattern through a series of questions that were centered on family and children. We found it rather interesting that EMF edged upward to questions we knew to be true and downward to questions we knew were false.

Normally, minor EMF fluctuations would be dismissed. In this case, however, they appeared to coincide with specific questions. We would have to pay very close attention in the review process to see if any EVPs were captured during this time.

The investigation continued quietly and uneventfully by both teams and was concluded sometime after 3:00 A.M. On the drive home, Bev and I shared the night's events and hoped evidence would be identified that would support our experiences. We were also eager to get started on the research.

A few days later, Matt and Melanie called. The news wasn't encouraging. They had found nothing on video or audio. Then, building bad upon bad, Matt informed us the thermal images did not download to the hard drive and there was no record of the handprints.

We were a bit discouraged until Bev remembered she had videotaped the thermal images. We immediately pulled up Bev's video. There they were!

After completing our evidence review, we were satisfied to have captured a few very curious EVPs. Two were recorded in the third floor bathroom. The first was heard after Melanie's team had left the room and were somewhere down the hall. The whispered voice says, "Hi Maggie." About twenty minutes later, another EVP that sounded like a different voice said, "He hit her."

Another audio clip captured on the third floor occurred at the time I was with Matt's team in the back room. I had asked if Emory was a coward for killing himself. At the time Jeff thought he'd heard a *"no."* My handheld video camera's audio picked up the very faint word, "No." After listening to it several times, we began to wonder if the word was "window" instead of "no." This evidence along with others can be heard in our Secret Room.

Our last EVP was surprisingly loud and clear, recorded in the basement where the shadow had been seen by Matt and Jeff. Melanie's group was in the basement at the time it was captured. The simple words, "see the chair" were heard. It sounded like the voice of a child, a young boy.

Normally, before an investigation, we do as much research as possible. In this case, we weren't able to do that because the Arlington investigation came up quickly. Now it was time to get to work and see if actual history will support the stories and connect the evidence of this investigation.

One of the bar's urban legends is that of the woman killed in the third floor bathroom. We considered the third floor EVP, "He hit her," might be related to this legend. Our search, however, did not turn up a murder. Of course, it is likely that some type of violence occurred between a man and a woman in the hotel's history. This is very likely knowing that, at various times in its history, Bay City as a town known for its prostitution, violence and criminal underworld.

As a December 11, 1917, article in the *Bay City Times Tribune* reads, the city was "being made a dumping ground for both men and women of the underworld ..."

The article continued, "...there exists in Bay City today a condition of lewdness and immorality calling for immediate suppression on the part of the authorities..."

There is also the ongoing legend that the hotel served as a speakeasy during the Prohibition era. We couldn't find anything that would indicate the hotel violated prohibition laws. Yet it is very possible. After all, during Prohibition, Bay City was a hub of illegal nightclubs and dance halls.

A January 7, 1921, article in the *Bay City Times Tribune* reads: "The flagrant violation of the prohibition law in Bay City and Bay County is a crying disgrace and an unending source of criticism ... It is commonly boasted that it is no trick at all to go into Bay City and if you have the price buy whisky."

Another of the Arlington's urban legends is the story of the bartender who either committed suicide or accidently fell from the third floor balcony to the main, first floor lobby. There is some truth to that story, though the person who died wasn't a bartender and did not fall from the inside balcony.

Earlier we mentioned a man by the name of Emory Fritz. The day we investigated the Arlington all we knew about Emory is that he had a wife, children and jumped from a third floor window. With additional research, more of the story was revealed.

By all accounts he was a loving husband and devoted father who had a good job as a railroad car inspector. Emory and his family lived just a few blocks from the Arlington Hotel.

On a hot Sunday morning, August 1910, Emory walked to the Arlington Hotel, registered and was given a room on the third floor. He told the clerk he was tired and wanted to lie down for a while. Just half an hour later, he jumped from the third floor window, his motionless body lying on the sidewalk below. The fall fractured his spine and gave him a severe brain injury. He never regained consciousness and died a few days later. The only thing Emory left behind was a short note that simply stated he had $15.00 in his pocket.

Emory's wife had no idea he had gone to the Arlington and could give no reason why he would be there. In spite of that, she still refused to believe it was suicide. She claimed he was likely sick, went to the window for fresh air, became dizzy and fell out. His death certificate indicates cause of death was an accidental fall. Why Emory fell from the third floor window remains a mystery.

Bev and I tried to identify what room Emory may have been in when he fell. We found an old photograph of the hotel taken somewhere around 1910. The only third floor rooms without obstruction were the last two rooms on the far right side. The other windows overlooked either hotel awnings or the entrance overhang. For Emory to have fallen directly from the third floor to the sidewalk below, he would have to be in one of the two last rooms. One of those was the room with the boarded window. The room where the handprints were found and the EVP that said "no" was recorded. Were the handprints and disembodied voice Emory Fritz?

"Hi Maggie," is another piece of audio evidence that, without a last name, cannot be connected to a specific person. However, there were two women by that name who passed away at the hotel. Each woman had a strong connection to the hotel and both were well known in the community.

Maggie Gainer was the niece of Mrs. Thomas Toohey, the hotelkeeper's wife. In 1886, at the age of 19, she came to live at the Arlington and served as a domestic. Maggie was an outgoing, cheerful young woman, well known and very popular in the Bay City community.

In the last half of September, 1889 she came down with a slight fever. Initially Maggie thought nothing of it, believing it to be a little virus. By the second week she was very ill with increased nausea, high fever, and chills. Maggie was diagnosed with typhoid malaria fever, a severe illness that combines the symptoms of malaria and typhoid fever. She struggled for five weeks, eventually succumbing to her illness in late October. Maggie was just 22 years old.

Another death at the hotel was that of Margaretta Wechsler, mother of Kate Hammerbackin. Kate's husband, Andrew, was hotelkeeper at the Arlington. Margaretta, known to most as Maggie, helped out as the housekeeper. Gentle and kind, with a quirky sense of humor, she was loved by all who knew her. Even with a weak heart caused by rheumatic fever, she still diligently went about her daily tasks. Sadly, she passed away in mid-April of 1910, from rheumatic heart failure. Maggie was 64 years old. Her passing was mourned by many.

The final piece of evidence was the voice of a young child, "See the chair." We began a lengthy quest to find some reference to a child or children who may have died at the hotel. If so, was it possible a chair held some significance to that child?

Researching this aspect of the story was not the easiest thing we've ever done. Weeks were spent searching through census, birth and death records, newspaper archives and communicating with people connected to the Arlington Hotel. That's how we found Eldon.

In the late nineteenth century, one of the Arlington Hotel's most prominent owners was the Toohey family. After Thomas Toohey's passing in the 1890s, his wife, Bridget, took over management. In time it became too much for her to handle. That's when Thomas' cousin, Peter Toohey, stepped in to help.

Peter lived at the Arlington Hotel with his wife, Mary, and their adopted son, Eldon. At a very young age, Eldon developed Rheumatic Fever. He survived the illness but was left with rheumatism and a bad heart. Crippled by his condition, walking was difficult and Eldon spent a good deal of his life in a wheelchair. He was a fragile young boy who looked much younger than his years.

In spite of his situation, Eldon kept a positive, happy-go-lucky spirit, which was admired by the townspeople and cherished by his parents. He was one of West Bay City's most well-known children.

It was the summer of 1906. For the children of Bay City, the biggest event of the summer would be a raffle drawing for a Shetland pony and cart. Over 15,000 raffle tickets were sold. There was more than one sleepless night for the town's children as the raffle day neared. That included Eldon Toohey who could speak of nothing else but the little pony for the months preceding the raffle.

The day of the drawing, a huge crowd of children gathered at Wenona Beach. One little girl was selected, blindfolded, and asked to draw 10 tickets. The last one drawn would be the winner. It was number 3292. A cry was heard in the crowd and everyone turned. This number belonged to little Eldon Toohey. This would be the happiest moment of his life. For the rest of that summer and into early fall, Eldon could be seen with his pony. For the first time in a long while, this wonderful prize enabled him to enjoy many outings he would not otherwise have taken.

As the summer of 1906 faded into winter, so did Eldon's health. He spent a good deal of his time lying in bed or sitting in a wheelchair. His mother and father did everything they could to restore his health. Sadly, in the early morning hours of March 28, 1907, at the age of 13, Eldon Toohey passed away.

Suddenly the words, "See the chair," made sense. Did we miss something during our investigation of the cluttered basement? Was there buried somewhere beneath the debris or crushed under layers of brick and stone a small, unseen chair? Perhaps a wheelchair, broken and battered with age that remained unnoticed for over 100 years … Eldon's chair, just out of reach?

There were other deaths at the Arlington, at least seven that we identified. Are their spirits lingering at the hotel? That answer remains a mystery. The evidence collected during our investigation with Mid Michigan Paranormal Investigators opens the possibility of paranormal activity at the Arlington Hotel. Future investigations might eventually reveal exactly who or what remains.

Story Seven
Harry Bennett Lodge

Lost Lake Scout Reserve
4930 Lake Station Ave., Lake, MI
Password: hpr2010
Investigative Team:
Hauntings Paranormal Research

It was a perfect winter day in Michigan as we turned onto the ice-crusted road of Lost Lake Scout Reserve. The sun was shimmering through the pine trees, reflecting off the glazed snow. Driving past the welcome center and small cabins dotting the tree line we finally arrived at Harry Bennett's Lodge. The lodge and scout reserve rest on nearly 3000 acres of forest.

This weekend Kat and I would be investigating the very remote cabin and hunting lodge of one of America's most powerful and ruthless businessmen, Harry Bennett. In the early days of the auto industry, Harry Bennett was Henry Ford's right-hand man.

He was a tough guy. Harry didn't have the usual degree in business management, but then these were unusual times in America and especially in Michigan.

The massive, 8,400-square-foot, beige log cabin was a striking contrast to the backdrop of frozen Lost Lake. Upon closer inspection, it wasn't a log cabin at all. The thick walls were made out of cement. A little strange, we thought before heading inside.

Entering through the small kitchen we noted 1930's style cabinets that appeared original, over seventy years old. Moving to a larger room we met Scott, the camp manager, who warmly greeted us and moved into the den by the fire. On one of the coldest days this winter the warm greeting and blazing fire were appreciated. The fireplace was enormous. A person could actually walk into it.

The main portion of the den contained rows of tables with folding chairs. Today the area is used primarily for presentations, eating meals and showing movies to the scouts. The room next to it was the original cabin, prior to Harry Bennett. Today, it is used to serve food, with several folding tables in the center, overstuffed chairs against the wall and a large piano in the corner.

There was a purpose to just about everything in the cabin, from room layout to placement of doors. Scott would give us the strange details later on the tour.

Our group would have the good fortune of spending two nights at the cabin. We selected a small room with two twin beds separated by an end table. Actually, the beds were very narrow, more like cots.

The rooms were simply furnished. Ours contained a bathroom, small closet, desk and table. Much of the original furniture from Harry's day still remained in the cabin. The rugged luxury of the furnishings is a little tarnished now.

Today the cabin is used primarily by the Boy Scouts. Oh, we should probably mention there would be Cub Scouts with us over the weekend. In fact, some scouts and dads had already arrived. They were having fun playing on the piano in the serving room. The perky little boys would make this weekend fun. We didn't know then just how much fun.

Once we settled into our room, Lorena Wygant, co-founder of Hauntings Paranormal Research, arrived with her team. Her co-founder, Dawn, would meet us at dinner. The members for this investigation were Jessica, Melissa, Doug and Tammy.

Since it was our first investigation with the group, I told Kat to behave. We wanted to make a good impression, so no silly behavior or stupid jokes for at least the first hour. Kat protested because her jokes weren't stupid. As usual, I ignored her.

Lead team members of Hauntings Paranormal Investigations
(L to R) Lorena Wygant, founder; Dawn, co-founder; Jessica, Investigator

Lorena was an active member of a TAPS affiliate while living in Las Vegas. Now, back in Michigan she got right to work and co-founded Hauntings Paranormal Research with Dawn, her long-time friend. Both ladies and their team have an extensive background in paranormal investigations. For now, they were fighting over who was going to get what room.

After everyone settled in, Scott stopped by to say he had to take care of some business. He would be back later to give everyone the grand tour.

This was the perfect time for dinner. Lorena knew of a great place for pizza. That's where we went, DJ's Bar and Grill. The pine interior and heavy beams lent a northern woods atmosphere, just what you would expect in this rural area of Clare, Michigan.

It was packed with snowmobilers, and conversation was lively. During dinner we all got to know each other. When Dawn arrived everyone was in a deep philosophical discussion over the pros and cons of various soft drinks and pizza.

Later that evening Scott gathered all of us around the den fireplace. The tour of the cabin and its history was about to begin. To understand the cabin, however, a person has to understand Harry Bennett.

Scott (L), the campground manager, stands with Lorena (R) as he tells the group about the history behind the Harry Bennett Lodge.

The story of Harry Bennett and Henry Ford goes back nearly 100 years when they first met. Harry was a navy man known for his professional fighting and an all-around tough guy, not afraid of anything. There are two versions as to how they met.

One story has Harry introduced to Henry Ford in New York one day in 1915. Harry was in a street brawl when a reporter saw him. The reporter, on his way to interview Ford, was impressed with his fighting. Thinking Ford might enjoy Harry, the reporter brought him along so they could meet. Ford was immediately attracted to Harry.

The second story is much simpler. Harry's brother got him a job at Ford Dearborn, as a clerk. Harry made sure Ford knew he was there. Ford Motor Company was rapidly growing and Ford was not well liked across America. His radical social views and increasing demands on employees made him hated by many. He feared for his life and that of his family. It didn't take long for Ford to realized Harry was the perfect fix.

Regardless of how they met, Harry and Ford built a bond that lasted for decades. They were a perfect fit for each other and Harry was devoutly loyal to Ford.

The 1920s and 1930s saw a split in our country between fascists, many supporting Hitler and socialists supporting unionization. Ford had fascist leanings. There are even rumors he donated to Hitler's cause as well as many fascist leaders in the U.S.

Harry Bennett (L) and Henry Ford (R)
had a special relationship

Library of Congress

Ford was deeply admired by Adolph Hitler. Parts of Ford's four-part booklets, *The International Jew*, can be found almost word for word in *Mein Kampf.* Hitler also had a full-length oil painting of Ford in his Munich office.

Harry had similar social beliefs as did Ford. He openly supported Wm. Charles Pelley, founder of the fascist group Silver Legion, and Detroit's outspoken Father Charles Coughlin. Harry was always asking friends and business acquaintances to support their causes.

A likable guy, he had connections with the Mafia, Purple Gang, and other underworld elements in the Detroit area. He was also associated with many military and political figures, both in Michigan and Washington. Harry was perfect for Ford and placed in charge of personnel. He developed a service department. It was staffed with a blend of mobsters, fighters, athletes and tough guys. The department was known as the police force of the company.

The department also handled Ford's personal security needs and anything else that required the staff's special skills. Harry got things done even without Ford having to ask.

The service department was brutal. It monitored employees at work, beat or eliminated those with union sympathies, and even broke into workers homes on Sunday to make sure they went to church.

Probably the most noted event with Harry's service department was the 1937 *Battle of the Overpass* outside of Gate 4 at the Dearborn Rouge Plant. Walter Reuther and several union leaders were passing out leaflets to a large group of supporters. Harry's thugs arrived and started beating Walter and the others, including the women.

Walter's bloody face made front pages across the country and drew national attention. This battle was actually the beginning of Harry's slow demise and the catapult for Walter Reuther's rise to fame as a union leader.

Henry Ford's son and president of the company, Edsel, was expected to take his father's place as chairman when the elder retired. Ford always considered his son weak. In virtually every instance Ford would take Harry's side over Edsel's and was continually ridiculing and berating the young man. Edsel sympathized with the workers and wanted to negotiate with the union. After all, GM and the other auto companies had already accepted unionization.

This Battle of the Overpass photo appeared on the front page
of most newspapers. The battle led to Reuther's rise to fame and
Bennett's eventual demise. Walther Reuther is forefront, right, center.

Many believe his father's
abuse caused Edsel to become ill
in the 1930s. Eventually he died
of stomach cancer at his Grosse
Point Shores home in 1943 at
the age of 49. Before his death
in 1941, however, the union
was recognized by Ford Motor
Company.

There is no doubt that after
Edsel's death, Ford intended to
turn the company over to Harry.
Some believe he wanted to do
that even before his son died.
The two strong women in Henry
Ford's life would prevent that
from happening,

His wife, Clara, said she
would divorce him if Harry was

Edsel Ford sympathized
with the union.

given the company. Edsel's wife, Eleanor, blamed Harry for her husband's declining health and subsequent death. Her ace card: Ford stock. She threatened to sell it all if Harry was put in charge. Ford eventually caved in to the ladies' demands. Eleanor's son, young Henry Ford II would take over the presidency and eventually become chairman.

Finally, in 1945 young Ford called Harry into his office one day and simply terminated his thirty-year career. When the young Ford nervously told his grandfather what he had done, Henry Ford's simple response was, "Well, now, Harry is back on the street where he started."

After leaving Ford, Harry's life was relatively uneventful. He retired and moved to California, where he died in 1979. During his lifetime Harry had three wives and four daughters.

While at Ford, Harry was responsible for many beatings and suspect for numerous murders and disappearances; yet, he had a softer side as well. Harry loved children and doted on his own. Each time his daughters would come to the lodge he would have lavish parties and invite all the local children.

When his seventeen-year-old daughter Trudie (Gertrude) disappeared, his entire service department as well as the FBI went looking for her. He thought she may have been kidnapped. A couple of days later it was discovered she eloped with her boyfriend. When questioned, Harry's response to reporters, "She is too young to be married." Yet a few months later he accepted both into the family.

In another instance a Ford employee's daughter was kidnapped. Ford told Harry to take care of it, but before anything could be done the parents paid the ransom and the child was returned. Strange, but two weeks later the ransom was recovered by Harry. Even more strange, the man suspected of the kidnapping was found murdered on a Detroit side street several days after that.

While at Ford Motor Company, Harry was well compensated for his service with good pay, readily available cash, homes and property, including the lodge on Lost Lake. However, Harry's ruthless ways put a target on his back. He was paranoid about his safety and took unusual measures to protect himself.

Harry surrounded himself with security at all times, and his homes were built as fortresses. An avid outdoorsmen and hunter, the lodge on Lost Lake was a safe refugee that only his daughters and close friends knew about. With this in mind, what Scott told us brought everything into perspective.

Scott started with the large room that was actually the original cabin. Harry built the house around this room. Today it is used to serve food. In the 1930s this large open room may have been used for dining, parties and entertainment. It has a few chairs along the walls, piano and serving tables. The doors in the outer, paneled wall blend into the paneling making them difficult to see, especially for intruders.

The den fireplace everyone kept huddling around had a dual purpose for Harry. Besides warming the room, inside the fireplace there were hand grips. If an enemy came, he could climb up the chimney, onto the roof, down the building to the lake. There he kept a boat to cross the water to his private airstrip. The cabin's window glass was about three inches thick making the windows virtually bullet proof.

The table in the back of the den has a secret top where guns and rifles were stored. At that point, Scott pulled out a thick,

The fireplace had a secret escape route for Harry.

curved iron stake. He explained that when Harry built the lodge he also constructed a moat around it, filled with water. Stakes like the one he was holding were placed in the moat. If an enemy jumped in the water, he would certainly get the point that he was not welcome. The one bridge to cross over to the cabin was wired with dynamite. The moat has since been filled in and, naturally, the dynamite removed from the bridge.

Spikes were inserted in the mote for protection.
The license plates are from cars at the bottom of Lost Lake.
What do these cars hold?

Armed guards patrolled the 2900 acres, and guards were also stationed on the roof fitted with machine gun turrets. Harry acquired the turrets from his military friends. The roof also had a barbeque grill in the chimney, connected to the den's fireplace. The grill was used for entertaining and could be pulled out if Harry needed to escape from the den. Yes, Harry was a little concerned about his safety.

Throughout the cabin were secret or trap doors, tunnels and passageways that would help Harry make that quick get-a-way to the lake. In fact, every bedroom had at least two exits. Some doors in the lodge opened inward, some outward to confuse any unwanted guests.

Scott took us to the large master bedroom, adjacent to the room Harry's daughters used. When the daughters weren't there, his girlfriends used the room. Between the two bedrooms was a bathroom. Maybe that explains the heart-shaped tub.

With everyone crammed into the bathroom, I stepped out to get some photographs. Suddenly there was a loud boom. Going back in I heard Kat say, "No, don't anybody help me out. I'm okay really." Wanting to get a close-up video, she leaned over the tub and had a little slip and fall. On her way down Kat grabbed the shower curtains bringing them down on top of her. Tra la.

Now it was time to see the basement, which has two levels that can be accessed. Scott claims there could be six or more levels. Scott mentioned tunnels that lead out to the grounds from Harry's rum running days and who knows what else.

The first level of the basement is where Harry did a lot of entertaining, especially in the summer because it was cooler. Overstuffed chairs and small tables for playing poker filled one room. The library walls were lined with bookshelves, now empty, but once covered with volumes.

Against an outer wall is a large, high-voltage cupboard. Harry had a special electrical cable that ran out to the boat on a pulley. If he needed to escape in the boat, pull-starting an outboard motor

Harry spent a lot of time entertaining and playing poker in the basement.

Secret stairs
leading to sub-basement.

Bennett's Lodge has several
tunnels and secret passageway's
according to Scott.

could take time. Supposedly the boat was rigged to start with the electrical cable that would release as he sped across the lake.

Going to one bookcase, Scott reached under a shelf, pulled a little pin, and the case swung open to reveal the stairs leading to the secret sub level. Each step was a different size to make it awkward to travel up or down. Another intentional safety feature.

The second level was special to Harry. Story has it that at least two people, a former mistress and a gentleman by the name of Charlie were murdered here. In fact the main area is referred to as Charlie's Chamber. We couldn't find any proof of that happening. In fact, our research pulled up little information about people who visited and what actually went on there. This was, after all, Harry's private sanctuary.

To the left in Charlie's Chamber is a tunnel that leads to the lake. Now it is blocked off, but Harry planned to use it as an escape route to reach his boat if necessary.

One more very important aspect of this secret sub level is connected to Harry's pool. Frequently, when inviting friends over, especially the ladies, he wouldn't mention the pool. They would come to visit during hot summer days, without bathing suits. That wasn't a problem. Nasty Harry would tell the ladies the men would spend the day in the woods hunting and they could swim without suits.

What didn't nasty Harry tell the women? Harry and his friends would actually sneak into this level of the basement. He had a one-way mirror installed between the basement wall and pool. While the women were swimming, nasty Harry and his buddies would be drinking, smoking cigars and enjoying the view. Several prominent women stayed at the Bennett Lodge. One such guest was actress and Olympic swimmer, Esther Williams. We wonder if she ever used the pool.

Traveling through the lodge, Scott mentioned various areas where paranormal activity seems to exist. He told us reports have come from just about everywhere. People hear footsteps and voices in the halls and rooms. Light turn on and off. Shadows are seen throughout the cabin.

Lost Lake also seems to have ghostly activity. Scott was referring to a couple of things. The first revolves around the *lady of the lake*. There is a story about a group of people, including a mother and her son who were boating one day. Suddenly the boy fell in the water. Frantic, the woman jumped in to save her son. She searched and searched

What lives have been lost in the lake?

but couldn't find him. Tragically, mother and son died. Now, at night people claim to hear the woman searching for her son.

The other story is strangely fascinating. Harry would get a new company car every year. That's not unusual, but the bizarre thing is the special ritual he went through with the old car. The doors were welded shut; the vehicle was riddled with bullets and then dumped in the lake. Curiosity seekers have discovered four cars and there may be more still undiscovered in the silt clouded waters.

The bullet holes and welded doors may be so the cars couldn't be used again, or just another paranoia. It is also possible Harry had a much darker and violent idea. Kat and I have to wonder if there isn't something or someone inside those steel coffins at the bottom of the very dark and murky Lost Lake. That was a time in Detroit when many union members and sympathizers or gangsters suddenly went missing.

The entire lodge was fascinating and mysterious with secret doors and tunnels, so that when Scott said good night everyone was ready. The investigation began immediately and would cover two nights.

Earlier, Hauntings Paranormal positioned cameras and audio records in the basement, main rooms and hallways. We were divided into two groups. Kat would be with Jessica, Melissa and Tammy the first night. Lorena, Dawn, Doug and myself made up the second team. We were off.

Jessica's team and Kat started in the bedrooms, while Lorena took us into the den. Jessica's group covered each room, beginning with Harry's master bedroom. Kat and the others half-expected to see or hear something. There was a certain electricity in the dim room. At one point the conversation changed to laughing about the furniture and Harry in general. Then, back to a more serious tone. They watched and waited, continually talking to Harry asking for a response. They left the room with nothing.

The foursome methodically moved from one area to the next until the shift was over. For more than an hour they pleaded with the spirits to materialize or give some sign of their presence. Jessica offered words of encouragement. She would be happy to give a message to loved ones. The spirits were asked to talk into the devices (audio recorder, EMF meter and K2 meter) with the lights.

Sitting quietly there were times EMF showed life and that would keep everyone alert. Kat's video camera constantly scanning each room just in case. Eyes and ears strained in the stillness. However, that night was a bit disappointing.

Lorena's team went straight for the den and I brought up the rear dragging along my three cameras and equipment bag, banging into everything I passed. Why doesn't Kat ever have that problem with her equipment?

Shortly after settling down in the dark, Doug felt a cool breeze. Moving to his side Lorena noticed it. Hauntings Paranormal is very thorough when investigating. After a few minutes on their knees under tables, a heat vent was discovered in the wall.

Yet, while in the den, a few odd things did happened. Several sharp bangs were heard against the window. Not really responding to any questions, it was probably a critter outside or ice falling off the roof, but we still had to wonder about that.

A little later Lorena called out that she heard a man singing. Except for me, the others heard it too. Let's hope an audio recorder caught the singer. Early on, Dawn felt nauseous and also claimed her video camera was losing focus. Focus can be lost when moving a video camera too quickly, especially in the dark. That could be the reason, but maybe there was more to it. About the same time Lorena also felt a chill running down one arm. Temperature readings remained steady. Still, it really seemed like we were not alone.

All night long and into the morning, each team moved throughout the building. By the time we finished, the little hand on the clock was just past 4:00 A.M. Everyone wrapped things up and headed off for some much needed sleep. A little after 4:30 Kat and I crawled onto our cots. What a relief to know we could sleep in late and not worry about checking out by 11:00 A.M.

We awoke a few hours later, 7:45, to a rousing Billy Joel rendition of, no wait, that wasn't Billy Joel. It was a nightmare. No, that wasn't it either. Actually the piano, out in the serving room, was exploding with notes from the twenty or so scouts banging on the keys waiting for breakfast. They were just as perky this morning as they were last night. Well, three hours sleep was all we needed.

Just then, Lorena stuck her head in our room. "I saw a man in a blue shirt in the hallway last night and it wasn't Doug." Doug was wearing an orange shirt and was in his bedroom at the time. Kat being curious had Lorena describe the sequence of events.

Lorena had never experienced anything like that before. Was it an apparition? Suffering from sleep deprivation my response was, "Whatever."

With heads that felt like there should be a couple of empty bottles in our room, Kat and I joined the scouts along with the rest of our group in the outer area. The little guys were just so happy and friendly we had to love them. We also cried for joy when they left to go trekking through the woods.

Driving back to the lodge, it would be another gorgeous day in the wild. By afternoon Doug, Mellissa, Kat and I headed out to try and find the moat, while getting some photo and video of this pristine land. The brilliant sun warmed the air to a blistering 12 degrees. The best place to get a picture of the lodge was the parking lot; however, the lot was a sheet of ice from the cars and snowmobiles.

I have never been a graceful person, so outside shots of the building would wait for tomorrow. When we left I could get photos from the car. Dads, scouts and ice fishermen were dropping like

Kat, Doug and Melissa went to explore on the other side of the bridge.
Every step they took was on ice-crusted snow.

flies. Kat was more adventurous. Out she goes and down she goes. I wasn't going out there to help, but the man who fell right next to her came to Kat's rescue.

Walking across the snow (much easier than ice), I was laughing so hard at Kat's graceful flop, my eyes were tearing. That's probably why I didn't see the snow pile I dove into head-first. This time Doug pulled me out and it was their turn to laugh.

After exploring the grounds, bridge and moat area, now filled in, the four of us decided to go up to the roof. Naturally every step was covered in ice. Doug saved us all. Once on top the view was breathtaking. We could see ice fisherman out on the lake, scouts and dads snowmobiling and nothing else but acres of trees. The view must be awesome in the summer.

We also noticed the barbeque grill in the chimney. The grill Harry used for entertaining guests or as a secret escape route from the fireplace in the den. Today the scouts have added a shingled peak to the roof. Still, it's easy to see where the machine guns were positioned. Melissa crawled under the roof's peak to explore. The original cement was still there covered with leaves.

Next we moved to the back of the house for a better view of the lake and 127-foot screened porch. Harry spared no expense. At that point it was time to go inside and thaw since our eyes had frozen open. The scouts were returning for their spaghetti dinner and invited us to join. As night approached the scouts left for their cabins and it was back to work.

For the second night everyone stayed together moving carefully from one area to the next. In the hall by the bedrooms, the EMF flew clear up to 14, then 17. What was it? Either we were with a very strong presence or the walls were bleeding electricity. After careful inspection, unfortunately, it was the later so onward we moved.

A significant amount of time was spent in the lower basement levels, even though it was bitterly cold at around 35 degrees on the first level. Kat went down to the second level by herself for 15 minutes or so. The temp registered 17 and the light switch had frost on it.

Yet, for some reason she felt compelled to stay awhile. She was talking to the spirits and calling out to see if Charlie was there. He was the man supposedly killed in that room. Staying much longer than she expected, Kat moved up to where the rest of us were investigating.

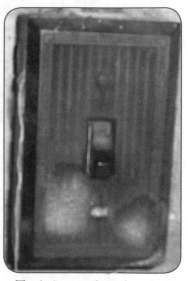

Later, when asked why she was down there so long Kat had her reasons. Only able to see a couple of inches in front of her, she thought something or someone was down there with her and was trying to call it out. Kat also didn't realize how long she was down there, until she checked her watch. It was almost as if she lost time.

The light switch in the sub-basement had frost on it.

Our group stayed on the first level for quite awhile. Again, sitting in the dark, Lorena began with some questions followed by silence waiting for a response. It felt a little strange sitting on Harry's old furniture trying to reach out to him.

At one point Lorena felt a chill down her back and left arm. Then she jumped slightly when she thought her pant leg moved. Yet the temperature remained a consistent 45 degrees with little change in EMF. Camera and audio batteries died. Nothing ever came. We assumed most of these occurrences were due to the cold.

Then the oddest thing happened. Jessica, sitting by an outer wall, became very warm. Her hands were actually hot. Extending her arm about a foot from the outer wall Kat could feel the cold pouring in. General opinion is that when a spirit is present they draw energy from their surroundings so people begin to feel a chill. Why Jessica was warm we couldn't understand, especially because the basement was chilly. Was there someone with us or not?

Eventually we cautiously descended down the uneven steps to the black, frigid sub-level. There was something ominous about

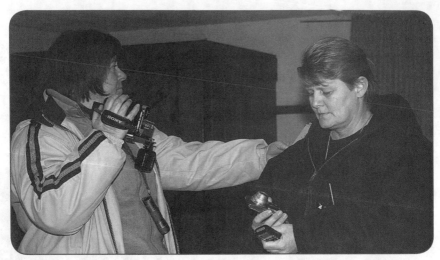

Kat checked EMF levels around Lorena, who was feeling chilled.

that lower room, our voices falling flat against the thick cement walls. We were constantly looking over our shoulders and peering into the depths half expecting someone to come out of a corner and touch us.

Maybe it was because of the tunnel that led to the lake. It was blocked off, but still, could there be something waiting inside? Whatever the reason, I know what Kat meant before; it didn't feel like we were alone. With the biting cold we left after about fifteen minutes.

At 4:30 Lorena called it a wrap. We headed off to our rooms. Whether we captured any evidence or not, Lost Lake Scout Reserve and Harry Bennett's cabin were a truly unique experience.

The next morning we packed up to go home. We hated to say goodbye to our new friends from Hauntings Paranormal Research. They are a very professional and friendly group who were great to work with; yet, exhausted, it would feel good to be home. So Cheese Nose and I bid farewell and headed out.

I know we have said this before, but we are saying it again. Reviewing the material we collected was an arduous experience. There were literally hours upon hours of video and audio to go over. Hauntings Paranormal had a whole lot more than we did. It took weeks for all of us to get through everything.

Naturally the first thing to be reviewed were the photographs, then video material. Nothing was discovered. Rarely do photos and video produce evidence; yet, there have been times, so everything is carefully examined.

The last thing we go through is audio, simply because it is the hardest to review. There is nothing to look at except static lines on a computer. After spending hours listening, earphones start hurting and then come the headaches. Hauntings Paranormal Research, Kat and I review all evidence, including audio, at least twice. That's a lot of headaches.

With the Harry Bennett Lodge at Lost Lake, the headaches were well worth it. We never expect to get evidence, yet there was just something unusual about our time at the lodge. We never felt like we were alone. It was as if someone was constantly watching. Also, there were several strange incidents that we all calked off as nothing, but could there be something to them?

Finding EVPs was really not a surprise, but some of the words were more than we expected. All of the following and more can be found in the secret room on our Web site. There were quite a few voices that were Class A and B, which means pretty understandable. Some are more difficult to hear.

The first night Jessica, Kat and the others started in the bedrooms. Taking a break from the EVP questions, they had some light conversation. That's when a raspy, angry voice can be heard talking over theirs.

The first few words are not clear. Then, "It's Monday night… I'll kill Lorraine." It was followed by a few more words drowned out by their voices. This is not the first time an EVP has been captured during general conversation.

Harry was known to lose his temper. Sitting in his room alone one Monday night was he angry for being stood up? Shortly after "Keri" or "Keriann" were recorded and "Hanrahan," possible guests at the lodge.

These voices did not seem to be responding directly to the ladies' questions. It may have been residual, something that Harry says every now and then while in his room. In a way maybe Harry was responding. It's possible that all the ladies in his room brought back old memories.

Another very clear voice is heard saying, "a@##**, … in here." The first word can be heard in our secret room.

That same night, in the den and outer room a number of voices were captured. Harry did a lot of business and entertaining at the lodge. He often had both mob and fascist friends over along with numerous ladies. On the first floor the most likely places for business and entertaining would be these two rooms.

The initial voices were captured during the period when Dawn was feeling sick and Lorena got a chill. Right around the time we heard the knocks that everyone assumed were nothing significant. What surprised us with these words is their relevance to the location.

In the first series a male voice can be heard saying "get out," "I lost a member," and "get out." Was Harry upset about losing a member of his service department? Later that evening "buy it" and "Freddie" were heard. A female voice calls out "playful" or "fateful."

In the original cabin, now serving room, a disembodied spirit declares "Help Dudley." Harry was a strong supporter of Dudley Pelley and his fascist Silver Shirt Legion. He would frequently ask people to support the man. Even though he's been gone many years, Harry is still looking for supporters.

Another voice retorts, "He got mean," followed shortly by, "has power."

The disembodied voices captured in the basement once more reflected the activities that supposedly took place down there. The cool, first level was used to entertain, cards and business on those hot summer days.

Harry could be talking about a girlfriend when this was picked up, "I got her the real thing." Maybe Harry bought his lady-love a diamond or mink. We also heard, "Like that," and, "I am already there."

During our investigation, everybody felt uneasy in the sub-level basement. Each one of us thought we were being watched and something was just about to happen. Maybe the tunnel made it feel creepy, or the rumors of murder, beatings and illegal booze. One thing is certain, this room was not a happy place and we could all sense that feeling.

The disembodied voices that were recorded in the sub-basement reflect emotion, fear and torment. They were at times very disturbing to listen to. They never responded to our direct questions but seemed to be words coming out of the walls in desperation. What the audio captured was, "Hiding," "Don't give up," "Not like this." The most disturbing was the last voice that whispered, "Back from hell."

Our long weekend at The Lost Lake Scout Reserve and Harry Bennett Lodge was fascinating. The grounds were pristine, Scott and the scouts were perfect hosts, and we made new friends with Hauntings Paranormal Research.

Sitting back now, we ask ourselves is the lodge haunted? Our many hours of questions seemed to fall on deaf ears, but there is definitely something there. As night dropped over the cabin we knew we were not alone. The disembodied voices that came out in the dark captured what Harry and his lodge were all about.

Harry Bennett loved the cabin. It was his place of escape for fun, quiet times and private business. Kat and I believe that Harry along with some of his friends and enemies are still there, back in the 1930s. They are still supporting their causes, fighting the union and having fun. This cement fortress was and will always be Harry Bennett's lodge.

Story Eight
Doherty Motor Hotel

604 N. McEwan Street, Clare, MI
Secret Room Password: krt48
Investigative Team:
Hauntings Paranormal Research

Today we were in Clare, a quiet, charming little town in the center of Michigan. Driving down McEwen we saw families walking down the street, peering into storefront windows. There was a little group in the donut shop. "Open Since 1896" read the small plaque on the building. Now it is owned and operated by a group of local police officers.

A block away, laughing people were leaving the Ideal Theater, where they had just seen a movie. Not a first run show but tickets were only $4. The theater crowd was moving toward the White House Restaurant. It was a small, old-fashion *hamburger joint* and the aroma from its hamburgers was wickedly enticing.

Directly across the street and seeming to tower over the other buildings was the Doherty Motor Hotel, the location of tonight's investigation. Its parking lot was packed and the hotel busy with all sorts of people coming and going for business and pleasure.

Yes, a charming town. If only this historic hotel could talk, what would it tell us? It was built in a time when the city was the state's leader in oil production and much more prosperous. A time when the Mafia and Purple Gang, enjoying luxury and wealth, flocked to the city to conduct their business deals in the shops and hotel.

Early Doherty Hotel attracted those who appreciated luxury.

Courtesy of The Doherty Motor Lodge

For decades people have believed there are those from the past who remain at the hotel. Spirits that just won't leave. We have to wonder if at least one of the spirits isn't from the murder that occurred in the bar over 75 years ago. Was it a gangland hit or just a crazy drunk?

Could some of the spirits be the Doherty family, family who have passed on but continue to love the hotel in death as much now as they did in life? It could even be the energy of former employees or guests. We were hoping to find out tonight.

The hotel has been owned and operated by the Doherty family since 1924 when Senator Alfred J. Doherty officially opened this grand lodging. It was passed on to his son and then his grandson, Alfred J. Doherty III who took over the reins in 1969. Today Dean and Jim Doherty, manage the hotel started by their great grandfather.

During prohibition in the 1920s and 1930s, Clare was home to the Purple Gang. Even the Mafia could be seen making backroom deals in many of the shops. In fact, Al Capone frequented some of these buildings; yet, the Purple Gang really owned the city. The Purples were one of Michigan's most notorious and dangerous criminal elements. They made their money in a variety of ways, but most notable was stealing illegal liquor shipments from other gangs.

The Purples, Russian Jewish immigrants, started in Detroit's Eastern Market region. How did they get their name? Well, legend has it that two vandalized shopkeepers were talking one day. One man said to the other, " These boys are not like other children… they're tainted, off color." "Yes", replied the other man, "They are rotten, purple, like the color of bad meat. They are a purple gang." From there the name just stuck.

With Clare being so rich from oil, it attracted the underworld. The Purple Gang moved into the area and spent much of their time at the Doherty Hotel. That leads us to the hotel's most noted death, a murder.

In the 1930s, two cousins, Jack Livingston and Isaiah Leebove, ended up in Clare as business partners. Livingston was a land leaser for oil and invited his cousin Leebove, an attorney for the mob, to join him. Leebove did a lot of criminal cases for the Purples and was tired of defending their petty crimes. On his way to Clare, Leebove was told to connect with a man by the name of Garfield from Detroit. He was the clean face of the mob. After the meeting, Garfield moved his operations to Clare.

Leebove started Mammoth Oil in the early 1930s and in 1933 Garfield joined the company. It was mob-run but, since they paid taxes, considered a legal business. This *legal* business also made it easy for them to run their gambling, prostitution and liquor operations without notice. The company did very well.

Leebove, Garfield and Livingston regularly frequented the lavish Doherty Hotel. These men weren't feared members of a violent gang but rather well known, respectable businessmen in the community. The hotel became their place to hold business meetings. According to A.J. Doherty, one reason meetings were held at the hotel was because it was one of the few places with a phone.

Things were going very well for these three gentlemen. Then a strange and tragic twist occurred on Saturday, May 14, 1938. There are numerous and conflicting articles about the events that evening, but some things are certain.

On that evening Livingston was having a drink seated in the center of the Doherty bar, then called the Grill Room. At some point he left to go to his room in the hotel.

Isaiah Leebove

Courtesy The Cleveland Plain Dealer, 1938

Jack Livingston

Courtesy The Seattle Daily Times, 1938

In a booth along the northwest corner of the Grill Room, Leebove was seated with Pete Geller, formerly from the Michigan

Attorney General's office and his wife, Elizabeth. There may have been one other person at the table, either Leebove's wife, Enida, or a business acquaintance.

They were enjoying drinks with lively conversation. Life and business was good. They didn't have a care in the world. No one suspected anything was wrong. No one noticed that Livingston had returned to the restaurant. Even if they saw, it wasn't a big deal. He was always there and he was a partner in Mammoth Oil.

Scene of the Leebove murder (photo circa 1930)

It was slightly after 10:00 P.M. when Livingston walked in, drunk, in a rage and carrying a gun. Taking the revolver, he walked directly over to their table, pointed the gun at Leebove and fired three shots.

According to accounts, Leebove was shot twice, with the fatal bullet piercing his heart. Pete Geller was also wounded in the attack. Leebove fell to the floor and the closest one to him, Elizabeth Geller, rushed to his side and put his head in her lap. Leebove's startled face looked up at Livingston. His last words were, "Jack, Jack, why...?"

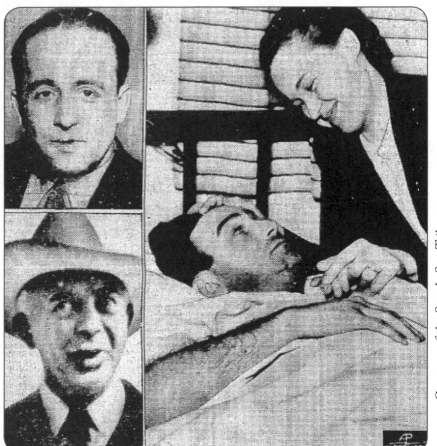

Leebove upper left; Livingston, lower left;
Geller in the hospital with his wife, right.

Then, Elizabeth Geller saw her husband on the floor. In shock and confusion, not realizing he had also been shot, she went to him and asked, "What's wrong darling." Geller simply asked for a glass of water.

Once it was over, without saying a word, Livingston just handed his gun to the assistant hotel manager. The young man took Livingston to his room where he calmly waited for the police.

Many in the community asked the same question Leebove had as he was dying, "Jack, Jack, why?" These men were cousins, respected and involved in a very successful company. People in

Clare liked both men and couldn't understand what had happened or why. Livingston would answer that question during the trial.

There are several theories as to why he shot Leebove. Livingston was a drinker. Some believe that with his heavy drinking Livingston had become paranoid, afraid Leebove was trying to cut him out of the business.

Livingston claimed that Leebove was planning a gang hit on him. How could his cousin and business partner do such a horrible thing after all this time? That fatal night in a drunken rage his fears and paranoia overtook him and he shot Leebove.

Others believe that Leebove had lost favor with the kingpins of the Detroit Purple Gang and they used Livingston to take him out. Knowing that he needed to kill his cousin and long time business associate he probably needed to get drunk to carry out this brutal murder. The truth may never be known. However, Livingston had three very savvy attorneys from Mammoth Oil defending him. They picked the right story.

Jack Livingston was fun, friendly and a respected figure in the community. In fact, while in prison waiting for trial he was released to give the commencement address at a local high school. Hard to believe that a suspected murderer was released to talk to high school students. That is indicative of the high esteem he held with the citizens of Clare. It is even reported that all the prisoners and guards at the jail thought he was a great man.

During the trial Jack Livingston claimed insanity. A long parade of witnesses took the stand to describe what happened that Saturday evening. There was no question that he shot Leebove. Whether he had good attorneys or just his charismatic nature, the jury found him not guilty by reason of insanity. People just couldn't believe that this man could commit murder. It was so far from his normal good nature he must have been insane. Livingston spent 90 days in mental rehabilitation then was released. Shortly after being release he moved to New Jersey.

Mammoth oil continued to operate very successfully for many years under the leadership of Sam Garfield. Most of the employees working for Mammoth never realized there was ever a mob connection.

Walking under the hotel marquee, we opened the doors to a small, but elegant lobby that has maintained its original 1920's elegance. Rich wood walls were still covered with original pieces from the early days, including an oxen yoke that was a favorite of A.J. Doherty. Leather furniture rested on thick carpeting. To our left was a banquet room and on our right the infamous bar where Leebove met his untimely death. Directly in front of us was a staircase leading to upper floor rooms.

Kat and I sat in the lobby as we waited for Hauntings Paranormal Research to join us for the hunt. We always look forward to seeing Lorena, Dawn and their teammates. They're fun to be with and serious about the hunt.

As we were getting our bearings, Lorena and Dawn walked in with their team. Everyone carried boxes of equipment, kind of like a paranormal caravan. Tonight, team members Jessica and Jules would be joining in the investigation.

Our tour guide for the evening was James Doherty, great grandson of Alfred J. Doherty. There was a certain pride in Jim as he talked about his family and the hotel. Over the years they have expanded the lodging to 157 rooms and added more conference areas along with other amenities, including an indoor pool and wireless Internet. Yet, through all the changes, the integrity and charm of the original building remains.

Their restaurant was full when we arrived and is known throughout the region for its service and food. They provide guests with breakfast, lunch and dinner from a very diverse menu.

James suggested we begin the tour in the basement and motioned to a door just off the main lobby. We entered into the first portion of the basement, which contained the men's bathroom. Recently updated, it was bright and cheerful. That would soon change as he ushered us into yet another door and a maze-like series of dark hallways and side rooms

Walking through hallways and rooms, we realized the basement was enormous. He brought us to a small room almost hidden behind another room. In the early days special guests of the hotel would use this room to play cards. At that point Jim was asked if the hotel served liquor during prohibition. He didn't know for sure but thought it was a strong possibility.

Turning down another corridor Jim pointed out that employees often hear voices and footsteps in these hallways. There is also a feeling of general discomfort and some think they are being watched.

The basement seemed to be one corridor after another.

Moving from one room to the next, we entered an area now used for maintenance and repair. It contained tools, work in progress and the like. The first floor bar was almost directly overhead. Glancing up to the ceiling, Kat saw two round holes roughly two feet in diameter, now covered. Holes in the floor, during prohibition, were quite common and used as methods of quickly and secretly bringing up or removing liquor from the upstairs bar should a raid occur. Well, the possibility the Doherty served liquor just became more probable.

This room was used for gambling in the early days.

Jim brought our group to a room near the basement entrance. Going in, it looked like a storage room holding artifacts from the past. We noted an old gaming table, possibly for poker, leaning against the wall. This is one of the tables that may have been used for those special poker games. An assortment of tables and chairs lined the walls, but something in the center of the room attracted our attention.

Holes in the ceiling could have been used to bring up or send down liquor during prohibition, in case of a raid.

Slightly removed from the other clutter was a wood and wicker wheelchair. Our entire group seemed drawn to it. We are not experts on furniture, but it looked very old, as if it could easily date back to the 1920s or 30s. When questioned, Jim didn't know who it originally belonged to but said the chair works fine. In fact, on occasion they have used it for guests needing assistance.

One of our last stops in the basement was the employee lounge. It was a small room with a large table in the center. Storage shelves lined one wall. Opposite the shelves was a small kitchen area. Jim mentioned employees often feel touched, hear voices, see apparitions and get the feeling someone is watching them in this area.

Who belonged to this wheelchair that seemed to mesmerize us?

We spoke to a young lady who was sitting in the room. She told us she is not scared in the room but did admit to hearing voices and feeling watched. It was just something she had become used to. No doubt the basement was intriguing and much time would be spent down here investigating.

The Leebove party was sitting in this area of the barroom on May 14, 1938.

Moving upstairs, our group noticed that many of the customers had left and it was much quieter. Jim took us directly into the barroom, the scene of Isaiah Leebove's dramatic murder. Jim pointed out where the Leebove party had been sitting on that horrible night in May 1938. In the past, the hotel has done reenactments of the murder. It is always a very popular event with the guests.

Jim mentioned there have been reports of apparitions and voices in this room as well as people feeling touched. Shirley, a bartender, laughingly described some of her experiences when alone in the bar. She emphatically described hearing voices, being touched and on more than one occasion felt a pinch on her behind. Without customers, who is the culprit? Could it be the bawdy antics of Isaiah Leebove, Jack Livingston or another of the bar's former patrons?

Returning to the lobby, Jim pointed toward the elevator and stairs. On numerous occasions the elevator has moved on its own, as if transporting unseen guests. When service is called, technicians can never find a problem. Here is another area where people have claimed to hear voices and see shadows moving through the hall and on the stairs.

A tragic heart attack ended one customer's stay.

Unfortunately, this is the location of a sudden death. With genuine sadness, Jim told us a guest had a heart attack near the elevator and no one was able to revive him. What was probably meant to be a pleasant night turned out to be his last.

We exited the lobby and moved down the hallway eventually entering Room 119. This is in one of the hotel's newer sections. Jim told us that one tragic night a man committed suicide in this room. The guest had not acted a bit suspicious but, the next morning, housekeeping came in to find him dead with an empty bottle of pills on the nightstand.

Jim had no idea what may have driven this person to such extreme measures. Standing in the room we could all feel a heaviness and sorrow. Could this unfortunate soul still be here?

Two more rooms were on our tour route. The first, room 280, where a woman died of natural causes. People claim to hear voices and shadows in the room and outer hall.

Our last stop was room 380. It belonged to Jim's grandmother, Helen Lucille Doherty. This had been Helen's living quarters for many years until her passing in 1990. Helen, loved by many, was warmly referred to as Grandma Doherty. She was an integral part of the hotel as was Jim and Dean's mother, Reine Doherty. There was special warmth in Jim's voice as he spoke of his mother, who passed away in 1997. He clearly felt a deep sense of love and respect for both of these two fine ladies.

The hotel was very busy the night we were there, and Jim excused himself to attend to guests at a banquet. Thanking him for his time, we were ready to begin the investigation. Lorena set up the base station in the basement. The investigation began in the basement allowing time for the upper floors time to clear out.

As mentioned earlier, the basement is an enormous labyrinth of halls and rooms. To get our bearing and also for baseline EMF and temperature readings we went through each area one more time.

While in the base station area we discovered something that drew our attention and fueled our imaginations. Behind a door, near the room used for poker, there were stairs. They led to a wall. Being courageous, Lorena climb to the top. Peaking through a slit in the wall she saw a small room behind the stairs. After careful examination, we think we may have found a locked door leading to the room. Still, we were fascinated by the stairs that led nowhere. Is it possible those stairs were used for special guests coming down to play cards, during prohibition? That's still a mystery to us.

Lorena checking a sealed-off room at the top of the forgotten staircase.

The first place revisited was a hallway that seemed very oppressive to everyone earlier. Kat and I felt dizzy and members of Hauntings could feel a tension, nausea and discomfort. Was this a spirit or not? We soon understood those feelings. Electrical wiring in this area of the basement created very high EMF levels. High EMF can often make people feel ill, light headed and create feelings of paranoia. Nothing supernatural here.

After our walkthrough, everyone divided into two groups. Kat was teamed with Lorena and Jessica while I worked with Jules. Lorena didn't want Jessica and I working together because she said we had a tendency to laugh and joke too much, not getting our work done. Not true of course.

Jules and I started in the area of the base station. To the back, there was a small, long narrow room. It is believed to be the place where secret poker games were held. With the lights off, this remote area was completely black. We couldn't even see our hands in front of our faces.

Our small team quietly sat, surrounded by inky darkness, as Jules quietly called out to the spirits. The only noise that of a humming furnace motor.

Suddenly there was an ear-shattering crash behind us. It actually took us a few seconds to recover. Apprehensively, flashlights on, we began searching for the sound eventually discovering it wasn't paranormal at all. Rather, it was a bottle coming down a chute from the bar. Even when we learned the cause, every time a bottle came crashing down it was a shock. Enough of this room, we moved on.

Our next stop was the employee lounge, where numerous staff members have had experiences. Before she even sat down, Jules sensed something in the room and I had to agree. We stayed in there for quite awhile talking and asking questions, half expecting a response. When it was time to leave, an audio recorder was left behind just in case the spirit was a shy one.

We exited the lounge just as Lorena, Jessica and Kat entered. Their time in the lounge remained relatively uneventful though there were able to identify the source of at least some of the unexplained sounds. The room directly across the hall captured footsteps and voices from the upper floor. These noises filtered into the break room creating unearthly sounds that were completely natural.

The trio next wandered into another section of the basement that contained the graveyard of forgotten antiques, artifacts. It is here the old wooden wheelchair sat. Its age was undeterminable though certainly appeared to date to the late nineteenth century.

There was something about this chair that seemed so powerful when we first saw it. Of course, there is always something about a wheelchair that carries with it an aura, a reminder of the difficult life someone spent sitting in this chair.

Kat walked with Jessica as she began taking the room's EMF levels. Approaching the wheelchair, Jessica slowly lowered the meter and the two women momentarily stared. The EMF immediately rose, fluctuating between 0.7 and 0.8. Jessica moved the reader around the area. It's levels remained normal until it approached the chair. For some crazy reason, the wood and wicker chair was generating high EMF.

Jessica (L) and Lorena (R) check EMF levels.

Kat called to Lorena to check it out. "Get that on video." Lorena directed Jessica. We stood and watched as levels slowly inched upward.

It is believed by many in the paranormal community that spirit energy can attach itself to furniture and other objects. The three contemplated the possibility of a spirit attachment to the chair.

Lorena asked, "Are you standing by the chair?" No response. "Are you sitting in the chair?" Again, no apparent response. EMF levels began to drop.

Kat pulled out her K2 meter and placed it on the seat near her audio recorder encouraging whatever entity may be near to return. Levels remained flat until Lorena asked, "Is your last name Doherty?"

Before she could finish the word "Doherty," the K2 hit, swinging from the first level, green, all the way to red, then quickly returned to green. A response?

The three exchanged glances. Lorena continued, "If your name is Doherty, would you please step up by the wheelchair." The K2 spiked 3 levels.

Kat asked, "Are you Mrs. Doherty, the one they call Grandma Doherty?" The K2 wavered a bit, a second light blinking for a moment before fading away.

"Do you mind me calling you grandma?" The K2 light spiked all the way up. Perhaps it wasn't the elder Doherty. Either that, or Grandma Doherty didn't like being called grandma by a stranger.

What immediately followed was a series of validating questions. The validation process is when a specific question is asked several times, in different orders, to determine if the K2 response remains consistent with each question. If responses are consistent, it confirms the likelihood of an intelligent spirit interaction. In this case, Lorena, Jessica and Kat were fascinated when their validating questions were confirmed. It seemed a communication had begun.

Lorena asked if the spirit could make a noise. It was strangely coincidental that the loud grind of the sump pump suddenly began. Lorena, chuckling and asked if the spirit had made the pump turn on. The K2 spiked again.

They asked if the spirit knew Jim Doherty, one of the Doherty Hotel's current owners. The K2 responded positively. When asked if the spirit would like to send a message to Jim, the K2 again jumped. Lorena and Kat looked at each other knowing the loud grinding of the sump pump would likely eliminate hearing an audible response, if there was one.

Using the K2's response, a series of questions revealed that the spirit was around 92 years old and had some attachment to the Doherty Hotel. The K2 responded positively to questions of a second female spirit presence.

When asked if the second spirit would come forward, Jessica's video camera battery suddenly failed. The trio focused their attention on the wheelchair as the questions continued.

Again, based on the K2 response, it seemed this additional spirit had entered the area and was communicating with them. These two spirits were related to one another, mother and daughter. The reason the mother and daughter remained together was their closeness and love for one another.

The K2 continued to respond to their questions for 40 minutes. Eventually the EMF levels and K2 response quieted. Whatever had been there was gone.

After the session, Kat stood somewhat surprised. It was the first time she had personally witnessed the K2 so consistently respond to questions. Lorena and Jessica agreed what had just happened was very rare. Though the basement was filled with a variety of distracting, natural noises, they all hoped some type of audio evidence would be identified that backed up the K2's hits and affirm the presence of spirit energy.

Jules and I met up with Lorena's group while they were still in the storeroom. We were sorry to have missed this rare event. Everyone stayed for a few more minutes, but the atmosphere had changed and we were now alone. Maybe something else would come up later in the evening.

It was nearly midnight, the restaurant and bar crowds were gone. We could spend time on the upper floors, including the bar room. This time we would investigate as one team.

L to R: Jessica, Kat and Jules investigating the barroom.

Moving into the bar most of the group sat at tables in the northwest corner. This was the spot where Isaiah Leebove was murdered. With the lights out the room was gloomy. The leprechaun murals on the wall, so cheerful and decorative during the day took on an eerie appearance.

Our main goal in the bar was to see if we could reach Leebove, Livingston, or whoever may remain. EMF, K2 and temperature gages would be used during the questioning, just in case something should happen. Joining us for a time was the bartender, Shirley, who had some prior experiences in the room. Almost in unison, everyone took a deep breath and the questioning began.

Kat started by asking Mr. Leebove if he was with us and if he had been an attorney for the Purple Gang. Lorena followed shortly after asking the spirit to talk to us. Nothing for a while, then the K2 lit up.

Questions continued in the hopes of getting a consistent response. The bartender, Shirley, mentioned that they sometimes had reenactments of the murder at the hotel. That's when I glanced over to see the K2's lights flash. Another hit.

Kat began talking about the history behind the Leebove and the Purple gain. During that time, EMF was monitored and remained steady, about .2. We thought things would remain quiet until the K2's lights again flashed in the dark room.

Shirley said, "Maybe he doesn't like it here because he was shot." K2 reacted again.

General conversation continued about the incident but, for a time, nothing happened. We began to wonder if the K2 hits were just random, natural energy elevations. Especially likely since temperature and the other EMF meter reading had remained consistent.

It wasn't until Lorena asked the spirit to have a seat with us that the K2 response began again., its lights sending us a quick flash. The presence was asked if it didn't like the table and would like another table. At that point all five lights went on.

The K2 meter along with a digital audio recorder was placed on a table more toward the center of the room. Had the original table the K2 was on brought back bad memories … memories of the shooting? Perhaps it wasn't Leebove's spirits responding but another former patron of the bar.

Lorena asked it to talk into the audio recording device. The K2 blinked. She responded, "Thank You."

Lorena trying to get a response

Kat, "Are you a man?" K2 blinked.

"Are you Mr. Leebove?"

Lorena quickly followed, "Are you the guy that was shot here." K2 hit.

Lorena asks if he was angry. Yet another K2 response. She asked if he would talk into the recorder then we could listen to it later, followed by "Do you understand?" K2 flashed again.

For several more minutes there appeared to be direct responses to questions. Based on those responses, it seemed we were communicating with an intelligent male energy who had spent a lot of time in the bar. He liked Shirley because she made him smile. At one point Shirley asked if this male spirit liked Jim and Dean Doherty. The lights of the K2 flashed brightly.

Additional responses from the K2 occurred when asked if it was Mr. Leebove and if he had been shot in the bar. Most of these questions were asked at least three times and validation was confirmed with consistent responses.

Our entire group sat stunned. No one had ever experienced anything like this until the Doherty. First direct responses in the basement from an older woman, possibly grandma Doherty, and a younger woman. Now it appeared possible Isaiah Leebove or another intelligent spirit was communicating with us in the bar.

We changed our line of questions. Lorena recalled that, earlier that evening, the K2 response in the basement indicated the female spirit down there would follow us upstairs. Lorena and Kat began to direct questions toward Mrs. Doherty. There were a few weak responses on the K2 but nothing strong or definitive. We didn't look at the minor response as significant.

As time passed, continued questions produced no results. Whatever may have been there was gone. We were alone now.

While the K2 hits were fascinating, we do not consider them valid evidence. Hauntings, Kat and I are not firm believers in the K2 because so many outside elements can generate a false response; yet, this was very intriguing. We would have to wait and see what the video, audio and photos would tell us.

Because of the activity in the barroom, we stayed much longer than expected. Checking our watches, we realized it was time to move on to the next location.

Since a man died from a heart attack near the lobby elevator and the lobby was now very quiet, we decided to place an audio recorder near that location. We had heard that the elevator is known to start and stop on its own. Though that could be an electrical issue, it wouldn't hurt to see if audio might turn up something interesting.

Everyone agreed our next stop would be Room 119, where the suicide occurred. We made our way through the newer section of the hotel and headed down the long hallway. Within minutes we stood in front of door marked 119. It was a pleasant room, with two full beds. A couple of chairs sat by a small table. After settling in, we began another EVP session asking specific questions to solicit a response from any remaining presence in the room.

Kat began, "We are calling the man or woman who committed suicide in this room? Is the person who committed suicide with us tonight? Can you tell us your name?"

A long silence followed. I asked how they killed themselves and we waited. During this period, Lorena was taking photos

The Hauntings Paranormal Research team setting up
and taking readings in room 119.

while Jessica scanned the room with her video camera and Jules checked EMF and temperature levels.

Lorena wanted to know why this person had committed suicide. Was it for love? No response.

Lorena asked again, "Did you kill yourself for love? Was your heart broken?" It is difficult to understand how desperate and sad a person must be to commit suicide. All of the questions asked were our attempt to comprehend and offer comforting words.

Lorena said she'd be happy to relay any messages to loved ones. Kat encouraged any spirit energy to speak into the digital audio recorder or move near the K2 and that we would be able to communicate with them in that way.

From the corner of the room, Jules softly spoke, "I see the name Ronnie. I don't know why."

No one knew who Ronnie was, but we decided to direct a few questions to him. Temperature readings and EMF levels remained flat. Was it possible someone by the name of Ronnie died in the room? It was also possible that Jules' sensitivity was picking up someone else. Of course, it could simply be the late hour and lack of sleep that can cause the mind to overreact. We just didn't know. It seemed our time in this room proved uneventful.

We had time for just one more stop, Room 380, Grandma Doherty's room. She had spent many years here. It was comfortable and large, with a king bed in the center, sofa and chairs.

Initial readings were taken. Average EMF was a very normal .4 with room temperature 74 degrees. Strangely, as soon as Kat turned on her recorder, the batteries drained. She had just put in a fresh battery moments

Jules senses the name Ronnie.

before. At that point we didn't know if a spirit drained the energy from the batteries or it was just a bad set of batteries.

The EVP questions began. Kat and Lorena began talking to grandma Doherty in the dark, a faded moonlight casting eerie shadows on the walls. They wanted to know if she was still here and if she enjoyed all of the changes that had been made to the hotel over the years. Questions continued for a good ten minutes followed by a long silence.

Suddenly Lorena let out a soft, sharp cry. Everyone jumped. In the dead silence and dim light her cry sounded like a shrill scream.

In a rushed voice Kat asked what happened as she quickly pointed the video camera in Lorena's direction. Jessica followed, also swinging her camera towards Lorena.

She stood completely still, non-responsive, her face expressionless as she glanced at each one of us. What?

Then a wicked smiled lifted one corner of her mouth and she shrugged. "Nothing. Just wanted to be sure no one was sleeping." With groans all around, sleeping we were not.

Nearly an hour was spent in the room with absolutely no results. The investigation had gone on for over six hours. It was early morning and everyone was exhausted. The group decided to wrap it up and head out. Now it was simply a matter of reviewing all the video, audio and photos to see what might have been captured. Hauntings Paranormal, Kat and I had our work cut out for us.

Several weeks later we had gone through everything more than once, as did Hauntings Paranormal Research. Parts of the investigation produced disappointing results. Then again, some of the evidence gave us chills. Video and photographs produced nothing but audio was a different matter.

In Grandma [Helen] Doherty's room nothing was captured and that was a little disappointing. Either she wasn't there or just didn't want to talk to us that night. Also, the elevator in the lobby never moved on its own and no electronic voice phenomena (EVP) were recorded.

While in room 119, our gentle questions tried to find out who he was and why he did such a desperate deed. At one point Kat ask, "Can you tell us your name?" A possible EVP was captured but its very soft reply is almost undecipherable. Kat and I believe it says, "Hatchin" or "Atchin."

A little later, trying to find out why he killed himself Lorena asked, "Did you kill yourself for love? Was your heart broken?" The clear, gentle response a few seconds later was "Emma." Now we were never able to get any information on the suicide, but hearing those last words truly saddened us. Did he actually kill himself for love or did Emma mean something entirely different?

At this time, our research has not identified anyone by the name of Emma, Hatchin or Atchin associated with this room or the hotel. Should something be discovered later, we will post it in our Secret Room.

Moving to the basement, where our investigation actually began, there was no video or photo evidence collected. The audio recorders placed throughout gave us little results except for two rooms.

One was the employee break room. This is the area where Jules felt a presence. There was a certain feeling I got, as well, when sitting in the room. It's hard to describe, but something just wasn't right. We left our audio recorders in the room for the remainder of the evening. After we left, I left my recorder behind.

About one hour later my audio recorder picked up the voices of Lorena's group as they began their investigation of this room. It was then, over their voices, that a clear, sing-song voice of a young child was recorded. It lasted for perhaps 10 seconds. Who was this carefree little one? Over the decades there have been many Doherty children and children of guests who have roamed the hotel. It seems at least one little child was left behind.

EVPs were also collected in a storage room not far from the entrance of the basement. That is the room Lorena's group spent so much time because of direct K2 responses. Was the K2 just acting up, or was someone really with them. A very old wheelchair was in the center of the room that drew everyone's attention.

There is no question in that dark and cluttered room they were not alone. There were a series of EVPs that seemed to match the K2 hits precisely.

Kat made a statement, "You can pull my hair a little bit." Then the response, "Help me."

Another voice, "Hope you stay."

Kat asked, "Are you Mrs. Doherty, the one they call Grandma Doherty?" The answer was "Betty." So this lady wasn't Mrs. Helen (Grandma) Doherty.

We began searching for any member of the Doherty family whose named was Betty. We finally came across the 1930 Clare census, and there she was, Mary Elizabeth "Betty" Doherty. She lived in Clare and the records show her living at the Doherty Hotel. At the time of the census, the young lady was fourteen. Perhaps on a future investigation we can direct questions to Betty and discover if it truly is Betty Doherty and why her spirit remains.

At one point Kat asked the presence to share their name and their mother's name, the answer "Vanesco." At this time, we have been unable to associate anyone with that name to the Doherty Hotel.

When Lorena asked for the spirits to give any other sign that they were here, the answer was, "Help me."

During the time Lorena and Kat were talking about what a huge job it was to take care of such a large hotel, the response was, "Yes, mercy."

A little later Kat asked if there was someone else with the spirit, the answer was "Cassandra." At this time there is no information on a Cassandra.

As Lorena called it a wrap in that room and our group walked out, the EVP, "Wish you'd stay," was heard.

It's hard to imagine who could be in the basement. We think Mrs. Doherty was present and a younger woman, possibly Betty. Research is still being done to see if we can uncover the importance of Vanesco and Cassandra. Hopefully one day we will uncover their secret identities. These EVPs and more are available in the Doherty Hotel Motor Lodge Secret Room.

Our investigative team had a lot of K2 hits in the barroom but had evidence been recorded that would support those eerie responses? Video and photos turned up nothing. Audio was saved for last. Listening to audio, the hiss of white noise occupied the space between our questions, but almost immediately responses began to come through and they were compelling.

When Kat asked, "Mr. Leebove are you here?" a male voice responded, "That's right, I'm here." There was a pause and then, "I'm happy."

Later, Kat again asked are you Mr. Leebove?" Lorena added, "Are you the guy that was shot?" The reply, "Yes."

Since Shirley, the bartender, has been touched, pinched and often just felt a general presence near her we asked him about Shirley. Did he know her, like her, pinch her butt and with each question the K2 responded. During that period of time there were also several "Yes" responses captured on various recorders.

After a K2 response Lorena or Kat would often say, "thank you." A surprisingly clear EVP was picked up after one of those thank you's that sounded very much like a woman. "Why would you thank him, dear?" The voice seemed very much like a prim and proper woman, with a slight British accent.

The clarity of the voice was startling and we wondered who she was. Was it Mrs. Geller seated at the table with Leebove or one of the many witnesses there that fateful evening? Then again, it could even be Helen Doherty not understanding why we would be thanking Leebove.

Perhaps the most stunning piece of audio collected in the bar, we believe, validates that Leebove was with us. I recalled reading 1938 newspaper clippings recounting the night of Leebove's murder. They all indicated that, after being shot, Leebove looked at Livingson and asked, "Jack, Jack, why…" His words fading as his life drained away.

Three, hushed words were recorded, "Tell me why?" Had Leebove just finished his dying sentence, "Jack, Jack why … tell me why?" Is he still looking for answers from Livingston? Some day we hope he finds the truth and rests.

So, is the Doherty Hotel haunted? We don't always give a direct answer. However the things that happened at the hotel were unexplainable. Our experience with the K2 coupled with the EVPs collected leave little doubt.

There are spirits at the hotel that don't want to leave for reasons we may never know. Isaiah Leebove, Mrs. Doherty, Betty Doherty, some happy little child, and possibly more are calling out, waiting for their next guest to arrive.

Story Nine
The Whiting

1241 East Kearsley St., Flint, MI
Secret Room Password: moy142
Investigative Team:
Mid Michigan Paranormal Investigators

I was involved in an intense project. My eyes were focused on the computer screen, my fingers flying across the keyboard when the phone range. Irritated, I didn't want this distraction. After the second ring, Bev picked it up.

I could hear her quiet conversation in the next room. Relieved that she was handling whoever was on the phone, I continued undaunted in my focus. A light tap on the door and there was Bev, phone in hand.

"What cha' doing?" She asked rather nonchalantly.

"Hmm, nothing. Working on a project."

"Really? Looks like a game of Zombie Killer on the screen."

"Oh. Right." I fumbled with the sleep button on my computer. Busted.

"What's up?"

"Matt Moyer is on the phone. You won't believe the next place he has for us to investigate."

Matt and Melanie Moyer are the co-founders of Mid Michigan Paranormal Investigators. A team we respect and frequently join on investigations.

"Where?"

"The Whiting."

Surprised I responded, "The Whiting Auditorium in Flint? It's a beautiful theater and relatively new. I didn't know it had paranormal activity?" With that Bev put the phone on speaker and Matt shared what he knew.

From Matt's understanding, there have been decades' worth of reports from Whiting employees. Actually, there is quite an assortment of phenomena including disembodied voices, shadowy apparitions and unexplained footsteps, to name a few.

No one is certain who may be haunting the auditorium, although some suspect it may be the spirits of at least two people who were known to have passed away in the theater. One is a worker who, during construction, fell from a scaffold on the stage. Another may be that of a guest who passed away in a lower balcony seat during a performance of "Oklahoma."

It is also the common belief there are other spirits, former employees of The Whiting, that may still remain attached to the auditorium. One of those is the long-time theater manager, Roy Bower.

This would be a very different investigation for us. Though we know a location doesn't have to be old to be haunted, our cases usually involve historic locations dating back to the 1800s or early 1900s. The Whiting Auditorium was opened in October of 1967, a baby in comparison to others.

It was a cold, blustery October evening when we met Matt, Melanie and team members outside the Whiting auditorium. Its construction was completed in 1966, but its first performance didn't occur until the fall of 1967.

The main lobby is quite impressive. A brilliant "Golden Sun" sculpture is suspended from the highest point of the sweeping ceiling. Seven feet in diameter and made-up of 675 gold-plated stainless steel branches, it was the original design of artist Harry Bertola. No one looking around this beautiful 2,000-seat auditorium would even suspect it might have its very own *opera ghosts*.

Theater elegance is highlighted with this brilliant gold ball.

Our guide for the evening was Wendi Fournier, Advertising and Promotions Manager for The Whiting. After introductions, she took us on a tour of the facility telling us some of the ghostly stories.

A few staff members, while alone in the theater, have reported hearing voices and loud footsteps down the empty corridors and stairways. Similar sounds have also been heard on the lower balcony.

Wendi Fournier, Advertising and Promotion Manager took us on a tour of the building.

Most reports, however, seem to focus on the stage. Several full-body apparitions have been seen and disembodied voices heard. As Wendi explained, there was a cleaning person who, late one night, came onto the stage and saw a full-body apparition in the doorway just to the right of the main floor. He was wearing workman's clothes. They believe it may have been the worker who fell to his death during construction.

For years, Wendi has attempted to research the death of this man but could find nothing in local newspapers. Her only thought is, at the time, no one wanted the Whiting's grand opening darkened by such a sad story. As a result, this tragic accident was intentionally omitted from the papers. Without a name or even specific date, it is impossible to research.

Fortunately, we were able to speak with a long-time employee of the Whiting, Ken Harris. He has served in various capacities over the past 39 years and is currently the house electrician. Before that, his father had served as a theater stagehand. If anyone knows the history of this place and what happened over the years, it would be Ken.

We asked him about the death of the workman. Though Ken hadn't been there at the time, his father had. In fact, his father was one of the men assigned to finish the job after the worker's

Ken Harris has been involved with the theater for a long time and knows much of the history.

death. It occurred sometime in 1966 or 1967, not long before the opening of the Whiting auditorium.

"It happened on stage left," he told us, motioning to the section of the stage that, from an audience perspective, would be the right side.

At the time, the crew had set up a suspended rigging system called a flying bridge. When it had to be moved, they attempted to reposition it in the air. Standing on the bridge at the time was a worker who stumbled during the move and fell to his death.

After that, The Whiting people had a very difficult time getting contract workers to finish the job. They ended up having the stagehands complete it. One of those assigned to the task was Ken's father.

Ken isn't certain if the theater is haunted though he admits to being spooked a few times. On more than one occasion, in the early morning hours, he's heard the sound of footsteps. Another time he watched as one of the large, suspended stage lamps began to swing, for no apparent reason.

He and Wendi both confirmed at least one or two guests passed while at the theater. One such tragedy occurred sometime between 2004 and 2005, during a performance of Oklahoma.

The gentleman was sitting in a front seat in the lower balcony with his family behind him. Sometime during the performance his head slumped forward. His wife and child thought he had drifted off to sleep. Sadly, it wasn't until after the performance concluded they discovered he had died.

Since then, there have been several reports of voices, strange sounds and footsteps in the lower balcony. Unfortunately, neither Ken or Wendi know this man's name nor the names of others who have passed while at the theater.

The most recent account of paranormal activity happened in November 2009. The theater had scheduled a Native American dance troupe.

Wendi was working in a back office when Doug, manager of the dance troupe, came in from the stage area. He asked if the theater was haunted. When Wendi asked why, he told her he had just seen a ghost.

Doug explained to her he was alone on stage and heard footsteps. When he turned around, no one was there. Thinking it was his imagination, he went back to the table on stage to pick up his bag. Again hearing footsteps he looked back. This time, to his shock and surprise, Doug saw the vision of a man, his face and shoulders clear. According to Doug, this person was wearing work clothes, including heavy boots. The two shared a silent stare then the eerie vision turned and vanished as it walked toward the back corridor.

Melanie, Matt, Bev and I were intrigued by these stories and eager to begin the investigation. Equipment setup began. Night vision cameras were positioned in the lower balcony and stage. Additional video was placed in the back corridor behind the stage. This is the section of the theater where talent stays before and during the performance.

As usual, the knowledgeable and well-organized Mid Michigan team had things setup and ready to go in less than an hour. It was time to go dark.

Bev and Melanie's group went to a back stairway where apparitions had been seen. I joined Matt's team on stage.

Matt began by introducing the group to whatever spirit might be around and asked if they would give us a sign of their presence. Extending the KII in his hand, he asked the spirits to communicate through the device explaining how they could do that.

Matt checks equipment and goes over the evening's strategy.

We waited in silence. Moments later, Matt mentioned he felt a cool draft. I had felt the coolness as well. I'd also heard a whisper to my left—the section called stage left. Matt scanned the area with his KII but EMF levels were flat.

Matt (L) takes EMF and temperatures readings with Rich (R)

About a hour into our investigation, we saw Bev enter the lower balcony. The battery on our audio recorder positioned up there was getting low and she'd come to change the battery. After completing the task, she quietly sat down on one of the stairs with her EMF meter and listened as Matt continued his line of questioning.

"Are you a steelworker that fell to your death?" No response.

Matt called out the name of Roy Brown, who had been manager of The Whiting for at least 25 years. Roy had passed away several years before. Some believed his spirit remains attached to the place he loved so much.

"Was your name Roy?" Matt's KII suddenly flashed red, the highest reading on the meter.

Michelle, a member of the team, said she'd heard a voice right around the time Matt had mentioned Roy's name.

Matt called up to Bev in the balcony to see if she'd said anything or heard anything. She told him no, but her EMF meter flashed to red at the same time Matt's KII hit.

That was curious. Was Roy with us? Matt asked Roy a series of questions, without obvious response or further EMF hits. It was a bit disappointing but not discouraging.

EMF fluctuations can occur naturally and don't always represent a paranormal event. It's only when the EMF consistently fluctuates in relation to a question that paranormal may be suspect. This segment of the audio would need to be reviewed for any response to validate the fluctuations.

Matt walked past the stage, just beyond the curtains, and discovered the cool draft was more obvious in this area. It didn't take long to find the culprit was a stage door with a poor seal. With things remaining quiet, Matt called a break.

Our group met up with Melanie's teams and Bev in the main lobby. I asked how it had gone in the stairwell.

Kat (L) and Melanie (R), in a lighter moment discussing the investigation.

Melanie shrugged and responded with a little laugh. "Lots of stairs. That's about it." Bev confirmed it was uneventful. They had remained in the emergency stairwell for some time. Then Wendi suggested they go to the upstairs office. This is the location where the scent of men's cologne had been smelled and strange scratching noises heard.

After a spending some time in the office, Melanie suggested they check out the basement. A door in the small administrative area led downstairs. Perhaps the scratching sound originated from some natural source down there. Heading to the basement, according to Bev, was when they encountered the scariest moment of their investigation. An incredibly steep, narrow stairway that was very tricky to maneuver.

Based on what Bev and Melanie said, the basement was one of the cleanest they've seen. Not even a stray spider web could be found. The grind of motors and roaring blowers made their time in the basement short.

Melanie, lower step, doing EVP work with Mari and Frank. It was very quiet.

The good lookin' guys of Mid Michigan.
L to R: Jeff, Frank, Rich, Matt, Aaron, Steve.

After a brief break, the investigation continued. The remainder of our time was spent in the main theater and stage area. The hours passed in silence. Oh how we wished ghost hunts were like reality ghost hunting TV shows. Shadow people, disembodied voices and crazy EMF hits from the *otherside* are a frequent occurrence on TV. Real paranormal investigations are not usually that eventful. Sure wish it were.

The investigation wrapped in the early morning hours. We thanked Wendi and the Mid Michigan team for allowing us to share in the hunt and headed home.

A few days later, Bev and I got down to the business of audio and video review. That's when we got the call from Matt and Melanie. We heard the controlled excitement in their voices and knew something was up. They believed they captured two shadowy apparitions on video. It was on the main stage. The dark shapes didn't appear to be reflective shadows from other team members, but they had to be sure. A return trip was scheduled to see if Matt and Melanie could recreate the scene in order to prove or disprove what was captured.

Our return trip was scheduled for the first weekend in February. Once again, Wendi was there to greet us, eager to see what would be discovered. Matt had the team reposition the cameras exactly as they had been on the previous investigation. He then attempted to recreate the position of team members and movements based on recorded video.

Throughout this time, Melanie sat at the monitors, comparing a replay of the previous video and providing additional direction to the team on positions. When everyone was in the right spot, the video cameras were turned on and the scene was recreated.

Was there a shadow on stage during our first visit?

Melanie's eyes focused closely on the multi-channel video monitor. We heard her mutter, "Oh, damn."

Matt looked over, "No good, huh?"

"Well, come see."

Everyone gathered around and watched as the video was replayed. Stationary infrared cameras reflected off the infrared light on one of the handheld cameras. This refracted light caused shadows.

Disappointed, Matt shrugged his shoulders. "Well, at least we identified the cause. That's good."

We were incredibly impressed with the way Matt, Melanie and the team worked to ultimately disprove the suspect apparitions. Not many teams would be so thorough, patient or willing to go to such lengths.

All too often we've seen teams eagerly accept the first video clip as *evidence* without any attempt to validate. It would have gone up on their Web site, Youtube and other media sources as their discovery; either for their own self-promotion and ego or just out of naivety and simple lack of objectivity. This is one of the reasons we admire and respect Mid Michigan Paranormal Investigators. They don't do that.

It was decided, since everyone was here and cameras were set, the group might as well run another investigation. This time, we were all on our own to investigate, no formal direction.

Earlier, Wendi had informed us that a few strange things had been going on in the Ladies Room. There was a recent report of a woman claiming to hear footsteps and the sound of a stall door, next to hers, close and latch. She didn't think much of it believing another lady was using the facility. When she got out, she was surprised that no one else was around.

Based on that, I decided to check it out. With video camera and audio recorder in hand I entered The Whiting Ladies Room.

What can I say about the Ladies Room? It's a very nice one. Clean, sparkling and in no way creepy. I walked into the center stall, the location where the woman had heard the footsteps, and closed the door. Feeling a little ridiculous, I stood there for some time in silence. I threw out an occasional invitation for someone to join me in the bathroom. No takers. Checking the EMF meter, I was surprised to see it reading more than 5.0. This certainly exceeded normal readings, which should be somewhere under 1.0.

I left the confinement of the center stall and walked through the bathroom. There were numerous pockets of high EMF levels. They were likely generated from electrical wiring and plumbing. I discovered that one of the room's highest levels was in the center stall. The exact location women had reported hearing the strange sounds. High EMF can have a variety of effects on people, including paranoia, nausea and confusion. I'm not sure what relationship, if any, the high EMF reading had on past reports, but I did find it curious.

I met up with Bev in the main lobby and we decided to head up to the lower balcony and check out the corridor just outside the entrance. This is another area Wendi mentioned where a few late-working employees reported hearing disembodied voices.

We entered through glass doors and slowly traveled the length of the hall. Blocked off by a glass wall on one side and soundproof doors leading to the balcony on the other, it was an unusually quiet section of the theater.

Second floor hall where people have heard voices.

Bev and I settled into a couple of chairs near the center of the hall, my audio recorder nearby. Over the years, we have investigated some pretty creepy places. This was definitely not one of them. The hallway seemed harmless and far from intimidating. After a few minutes, without apparent response to our questions, we entered into the second floor balcony. Bev and I took seats in the general location where the man was reported to have died.

I noticed my audio recorder was not on, so I hit the start button. Nothing. The battery was dead. What made this rather unusual is the fact I had put in fresh ones about an hour before. I wondered when it had stopped.

Quickly replacing batteries, I turned the recorder back on clicking back the last few seconds of audio. The sound abruptly cut off in the outside balcony corridor. Adding a bit of excitement to it, moments before the audio cut off the distinct sound of music was heard.

Bev and I glanced quickly at one another. Music? We replayed it a few times. It still sounded like musical notes. Almost like an orchestra or music box. There was no music in the whole theater that evening. In fact, the central speaker system was off. We made a note to check it out later. For now we continued our session in the lower balcony.

Our groups continued investigating, each moving quietly from area to area. Sometime after 11:15 P.M., Bev and I entered stage left, the back room and through the doors leading to the greenroom hall.

Doors lined each side. We walked into the first room on our left. It was spacious, lined with tabletop shelves, mirrors and chairs. Obviously the dressing room and make-up area for the general cast. Slowly we made our way from one room to another. Smaller rooms with comfy lounge chairs and private bathrooms were designed for the lead actors. Bev and I settled into one of these.

Taking the lounge chair I sat back putting my feet on the cushy footrest. Ah, this was very nice. A person could get used to a paranormal investigation like this. We sat there in comfort. Or, rather, I sat there in comfort while Bev perched herself in a hard

Kat triumphant in getting the comfy chair before Bev.

chair in front of the make-up mirror. I closed my eyes to her harsh glare. First one in gets automatic dibs on the chair. It wasn't my fault. Those are the rules.

We got back to the investigation and began a series of questions hoping to elicit some type of response. EMF levels remained flat, however, and nothing out the ordinary was experienced.

After several minutes, Bev got up telling me she wanted to check other rooms. Of course, I knew her real motive. After a few minutes, I got up and wandered into the room next door. She had found the other comfy lounge chair.

Reluctantly we left the area, returning to the main stage. As was the case with this evening's investigation, if there were opera ghosts wandering around this impressive theater it seemed they were keeping to themselves. Matt and Melanie called a wrap sometime after 2:00 A.M.

Evidence review is always a tedious, time consuming process. When all was said and done, however, Matt and Melanie, Bev and I were a bit surprised to discover several EVPs. Most, but not all, occurred around the stage.

On the first night of investigation, everyone was gathered in the main entrance taking a break. During one of our lighter moments we were talking about our favorite fruit, bananas (don't ask). At the end of the conversation a voice, not a member of the team, is heard, "I like bananas." Nice, a fruit-eating spirit.

Later, Matt was on stage with his KII and EMF meters. He was telling the spirits they could communicate through these devices. The responding voice says, "I see it."

This next occurred during the time Matt was trying to search out the cold draft on stage. A low voice whispered the name "Johnny". Of course, the name John or Johnny is so popular it's impossible to connect the name with anyone in particular. Who knows, perhaps it belonged to the worker who fell from the scaffold.

There is another interesting possibility. Wendi told us the Whiting was the last place Johnny Cash performed a full concert before his death. It's also where he first informed the public of his ailing health. Could the spirit voice "Johnny" be referring to the great Johnny Cash?

The next audio clip occurred on the second investigation. Bev and I were alone on the main stage. I had asked the spirits to communicate with us. At that moment, recorded on the audio, a whispered voice is heard saying, "Can I get out there," or, "Can I get out now."

Matt also identified a few interesting EVPs in the actors' dressing rooms. In Dressing Room #5, the words, "Damn it, damn it, damn it," were recorded. Sounds like the spirit of an actor having issues before a performance. Creative people are frequently blessed with emotional eruptions … damn it!

Another EVP, identified by Matt, was recorded in Dressing Room #4. It is a very clear, loud, "yes."

Perhaps the most surprising EVP occurred in the corridor outside of the lower balcony. The sound was heard shortly before my audio recorder's battery died. It was music, just as we thought. But even more, a single word was mixed in with the music. We believe it says, "Carousel."

There was a popular Richard Rodgers and Oscar Hammerstein musical called *Carousel*. Wendi Fournier did confirm that the production *Carousel* was performed at the Whiting sometime back in the mid-1970s or 1980s. Perhaps some event occurred during the performance that caused a residual energy to be embedded in the outer corridor. This residual energy now repeats itself again and again.

What struck us as even more peculiar was a second EVP in the same area. This one was heard shortly before the music began. It said, "…kill you."

There is no record of any violence occurring inside the theater. That, of course, doesn't mean some minor skirmish or verbal threat hasn't occurred.

Another possibility could be related to a scene in the musical *Carousel*. In this scene one of the lead characters, a guy by the name of Billy Bigelow, attempts to rob a wealthy businessman. The robbery attempt fails and Billy is pursued and cornered by the police. Rather than be taken and sent to jail, he kills himself. The words "kill you" could be one of the lines from that play.

Our investigation with Mid Michigan Paranormal Investigators gave us an incredible opportunity to investigate the beautiful Whiting Auditorium. Here, at last, is a good example validating the fact that a place does not have to be old and creepy to hold spirit energy.

Based on the audio evidence collected, Matt, Melanie, Bev and I believe there is considerable residual spirit energy embedded throughout the auditorium. Residual energy is very similar to an audio recording that is played over and over without thought or knowledge.

There may be one or two intelligent spirits hanging around, as well. Maybe they don't want to lose their free ticket to the next performance.

The next time you take in a show at the Whiting, keep your eyes and ears opens. It seems there is much more going on here than live stage performances.

Story Ten
Old Allegan Jail Museum

113 Walnut Street, Allegan, MI
Secret Room Password: hpi0051
Investigative Team:
Hauntings Paranormal Research

There have been ghost stories, of course. What respectable old prison doesn't have them? Stories of a spectral woman in the sheriff's residence, sounds of children who aren't there, and mannequins that change clothes either on their own or with the help of some ghostly visitor. More stories are told of those who have been touched or experienced odd sensations in the old jail cells.

There is definitely a collection of fascinating, ghostly folklore surrounding Old Allegan Jail Museum. The same stories have been written in newspapers and told on local radio and television stations along Michigan's west coast again, and again, and again.

Though ghost stories are always fun to hear for Bev and I, it isn't just about the ghost stories but finding the evidence that supports the claim. Is Old Allegan County Jail Museum really haunted or is it just part of the town's wonderful history and rich folklore?

With infrared video cameras, still cameras and an assortment of audio recorders and EMF meters packed away, we headed out in search of the truth. Lorena Wygant and her Hauntings Paranormal Research team would be the investigative group working with us on this short but aggressive investigation of the sheriff's residence and jailhouse.

Bev and I have worked with Lorena and her group before and respect their serious, straight-forward approach to investigation. We've also had some incredibly fun moments together and shared some hearty laughs, which always make an investigation more fun.

On the drive out to Michigan's west side, I shared some of Allegan's history with Bev. The name Allegan is said to come from the Native American tribe "Allegawi" or "Allegans" believed by some to have been identical with the mound builders. The county was organized in 1835. The region's dense forests and location along the Kalamazoo River made it a major trade route, and the small community rapidly grew. In 1907, Allegan was incorporated as a city.

Today, any visitor to Allegan must visit the historic downtown district. It is considered one of Michigan's best-preserved historic locations. Largely unchanged from its early days, most of the homes and businesses date from the early 1800s to early 1900s. The nostalgically charming downtown offers a unique variety of antiques and gift shops, restaurants, and professional businesses.

Of course, our focus was the Old Allegan Jail Museum. In 1906 it became the city's third jailhouse and served in that capacity until 1963. That's when the current prison, situated right across the street, was built.

The old jail not only housed prisoners but was also home to the sheriff and his family. The front, two-story section of the building served as the residence while the back, three-story building was the prison. It was built to hold approximately 31 prisoners.

Back in those days the sheriff's wife played an important role in managing the jail and its prisoners. She was usually given the task of preparing and serving inmate meals. It was hard work with long hours and offered incredibly low wages.

Over the years, the prison held some rather unsavory characters from murderers and rapists to the dangerously insane. The dedication of the sheriffs and their wives was remarkable, especially considering their children were nearby and not far from harm's way.

One of the more memorable stories in the jail's past is that of Sheriff George Smith. His life's ambition was to become the County Sheriff. As his career progressed, the opportunity finally presented itself in the fall of 1908.

The 1908 race for County Sheriff was a tough one. George put everything he had into running a strong, honest campaign. He ignored the constant, nagging cough he had developed over the course of the campaign. Thinking it was either an allergy or a cold he simply couldn't shake, he went to the doctor. The news wasn't good. He had contracted the white plague. Tuberculosis.

Determined to beat this deadly disease, George continued the grueling pace of the campaign. It paid off. In November George Smith won election. His career dream was fulfilled.

As November passed into December, George's cough became much worse and his health declined. His devoted wife, Lola, his son, Leon, and his old schoolmate and closest friend, Volney Ferris, were by his side. With his family and friend's strong emotional support, George Smith did not give up.

January 1, 1909, was the swearing-in day, the moment George had long awaited. He struggled out of bed, dressed in his finest and took the oath. George Smith was finally Sheriff of Allegan County.

The day was filled with joy and deep sadness. It was painfully obvious to everyone that George Smith did not have long to live. The disease had spread from his lungs to his internal organs. He passed away at his residence in the Allegan jail, March 3, 1909. The direct cause of death was kidney failure, a result of Tuberculosis.

Before his death, George Smith appointed Volney Ferris undersheriff. This was not a position Volney wanted, but he accepted the position as something he simply had to do. After his friend's passing, Volney assumed the role of Allegan County Sheriff.

George Smith's death was a terrible blow for his wife and son. Not only did they lose a loving husband and father, they lost all means of financial support.

Volney Ferris did not forsake Lola or Leon after his good friend's passing. One of his first acts as sheriff was to request every penny of his salary be turned over to George's family. Lola and Leon were very grateful and Volney quickly became a hero in their eyes.

Ferris held the position of Allegan County's Sheriff until 1914 and, later, served as a justice for Allegan County. He remains one of Allegan County's most respected, noteworthy historical figures.

I checked my watch as we neared Allegan. It was early, just after 4:00 P.M. We were making good time and would arrive a little ahead of schedule for this mostly-daytime investigation. It was scheduled to run just three hours, from 5:00 P.M. to 8:00 P.M.

Though the amount of time to investigate was short and a little unusual for most paranormal investigations, we certainly didn't mind. Bev and I realized that even three hours was an imposition for the dedicated volunteers of the Allegan County Historical Society. We were appreciative for whatever time they allowed us. Second, the two of us are not committed to the idea that paranormal investigations must be conducted at night, in total or even near-total darkness.

We believe that an investigation should be conducted around the time and in similar conditions as paranormal activity is most commonly reported. If it occurs in broad daylight or at night when the lights are on, investigate then and in similar lighting conditions. Since reports of strange phenomena have occurred at the jail all times of the day and night, a daytime investigation should work out well.

We pulled into the parking lot outside the old jail just about the time Lorena Wygant and two members of her team, Dawn and Jessica, arrived. It was really nice to see them again. We would have huddled, chatting in the parking lot for a while but the investigation would be short so we headed directly into the museum. Welcoming members of the Allegan Historical Society, Laura Ann and Helen, met us.

After introductions, Laura Ann took us on a tour of the facility that began at the front of the building, which is the area designated as the sheriff's residence. We have to applaud the society for maintaining, with meticulous attention, the residence in a nostalgically warm, turn-of-the-century style. Laura Ann explained that none of the furnishings, nick-knacks, pictures or other memorabilia were original to the house but, rather, donated items to the society.

Throughout the living quarters period furnishings have been donated to represent the nineteenth and twentieth centuries.

She took us directly upstairs where bedrooms had been decorated to represent different periods and styles of the nineteenth or early twentieth century. One room was setup like an old cabin with items from the old Whetmore cabin. The Whetmores were one of Allegan's earliest pioneer families. Another room was setup in the style of a formal nineteenth century dining room.

We were particularly fascinated by the many incredible artifacts and handmade heirlooms, including the Victorian hairworks. For those who unfamiliar with the term hairwork, it is a complex, artistic weaving of human hair into an intricate design. Hairworks were a very popular pasttime in the 1800s and early 1900s.

The hair used in the design sometimes came from one person or generations of family members. It may have been the hair of a husband or boyfriend who went off to war or it may have been made from the hair taken of a loved one who had passed.

Hairworks were made into jewelry or larger designs were framed and kept as a family heirloom. The beautiful hairworks in the home portion of the museum are some of the largest and most intricate we've seen.

As we returned to the first floor, I asked Laura Ann if she'd ever experienced anything unusual in the home or jail. She

Hairworks wreaths and art were very popular at the turn of the century.

chuckled lightly and shook her head no. She had been with the society for some time, spent many nights alone at the museum, and has never seen, heard or felt anything unusual. "I don't know how these stories start," she smiled.

On the main floor again, Laura Ann showed us into the parlor. It was yet another amazing room filled with a collection of historic

The parlor was filled with heirlooms.

furniture, heirlooms and Victorian memorabilia, including an old Edison record player and antique piano. Bev and I would have to come back another time when we could leisurely explore the rooms and enjoy the many antique collections.

Our tour of the residence ended in the big, homey kitchen. Here meals were prepared and served to the prisoners. A small cutout in the wall remained where the prisoners, who were permitted out of their cells, would come to pick up meals.

From there Laura Ann took us to the basement's laundry room. This is the area where prisoners, on good behavior, would be locked in to do the laundry. It was considered a privilege.

Hmm, who would think washing dirty clothes and ironing would be considered a privilege. Seriously, who knew? I have enjoyed this privilege all these years and never appreciated it. Kind of makes you rethink the whole idea of *good behavior*. Ah well, on with the tour.

This area offers an interesting collection of historical apparatus for washing clothes. Some of them looked downright deadly. Traveling on, we came to a room that had once been a storage room but has now been converted into a nineteenth century general store.

The Native American room is also located in the basement. The displays reveal a collection of arrowheads and ceremonial items. Finally, the very back room had been converted into a mock courtroom. Though not original to the jail, furnishings were taken from an old Allegan County courtroom.

We exited the basement and followed Laura Ann as she returned us to the gift shop, which once served as the original prisoner booking room. From there she ascended the old wooden stairway that would take us to prison section of the building.

Bev and I have investigated some of the creepiest prisons in America, including Eastern State Penitentiary, Ohio State Reformatory and Moundsville Penitentiary. Although the old Allegan jail is in excellent condition compared to the others, the eerie sensation still inched its way upward as we stared down the row of second floor cells. This had been the general population area designed for male prisoners.

The historical society had redone portions of the cellblock to recreate a historical village. One chamber was setup like an old dentist's office. I chuckled at the site of a child mannequin sitting calm and collected in the dentist's chair. It was looking rather *fly* with oversized sunglasses perched on its little mannequin nose.

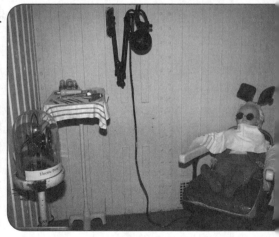

Cell representing an old dentist office.

Apparently the little dude was quite fearless of the dentist's drill. Another cell was set-up like an attorney's office, another a barbershop.

Of course, not all cells had undergone a makeover. Many remained untouched. Graffiti carved on the walls were a clear reminder of past inmates.

From here Laura Ann brought us to the third floor. This floor held women prisoners and the area designated as solitary confinement. One was particularly foreboding. It was the prison's designated isolation cell called "the hole." The hole held prisoners who were considered uncontrollable, either extremely violent or insane. We heard this cell was once padded. The padding, however, has long gone, and all that remains are brick walls and a heavy, solid door with a single peephole in the center.

Cells on the third floor.

This area of the prison would be a key focus during the investigation. Based on historical newspapers, the Allegan County Jail had held some of the state's most notorious criminals, including several that were considered violent psychopaths. If any place contained strong paranormal energy, it seemed these would be the most likely floors.

With that, our tour was over. We thanked Laura Ann for her time and immediately

Prisoners for the evening, L to R:
Lorena, Dawn, Jessica, Kat and Bev.
Would they be released early
on good behavior?

got down to business. Lorena, Dawn and Jessica began setting up the DVR cameras in the cellblocks while Bev and I headed to the residence section of the museum to begin private EVP sessions. I took the top floor while Bev remained on the first.

During our investigation of the residence, Bev and I must admit the atmosphere remained pleasant and completely benign. Nothing unusual or even remotely suspicious was felt or heard. Perhaps something would be discovered during audio review.

About thirty minutes later we met up with Lorena and her team. They had positioned cameras down the prison hallways and cellblocks, which were their main areas of video focus. Everyone was ready to go. Our group divided into two. Dawn, Jessica and Bev formed one team, Lorena and I the other. While Dawn, Jessica and Bev returned to the sheriff's residence, Lorena and I settled on the third floor. This was the floor where the women and younger people were kept as well as solitary confinement and the cell called "the hole."

Just as we were about to begin an EVP session, Lorena discovered she was missing a piece of equipment and headed downstairs to retrieve it. This left me alone for a few minutes.

I slowly walked into the different sections of the third floor finally stopping across the hall from solitary. The old cells in this section are filled with a collection of historical artifacts. I called out a few questions, attempting to solicit a response from any spirits that might remain. But, as so often occurs, a noticeable response was not heard. I returned to solitary and walked into the back cell.

Scrawled on the wall were the words, "I love Sue." I considered that for a moment and wondered out-loud if Sue loved him back. It was then I heard the sound of footsteps on the stairs. Lorena was returning.

Lorena suggested we begin an EVP session in the cell called *the hole*. She closed the solid door behind us and for a moment I felt the prickling sensation of claustrophobia. That vanished, however, when I turned to see the Halloween-masked dummy sitting in a corner. Cute.

Lorena checked EMF levels in the room then began the session. "We don't mean you any harm. We're just here to talk to you."

She continued with questions designed to get a response. "Did you like being in this jail?" "Did you die here?"

Lorena in "the Hole" doing EVP work with the dummy.

Pausing for several minutes between each question, we silently waited. Lorena and I remained alert to even the slightest sound or movement.

It was then a name came to mind, Elton Baldwin. He was confined to the isolation area of the Allegan Jail, the floor we were now investigating. Many in the community believed Elton Baldwin was West Michigan's male counterpart of Lizzie Borden. Elton was a non-descript, quiet man who lived with his mother in a rented farmhouse owned by the wealthy Whitney family.

It was a cold morning, March 4, 1909. Just one day after the tragic death of Sheriff George Smith. The community was still in mourning over the loss of their new sheriff. Volney Ferris, had just been sworn in as the new interim sheriff. Little did Ferris, his deputies or the townspeople know, Allegan County was about to be faced with one of its most sensational and horrific murders.

It was a little after 8:00 A.M. when the brutalized body of 58-year old Mrs. Mary Baldwin was discovered on the floor of the old farmhouse. She lay facedown down near the bed. Blood seeped from the ugly gouges in her head forming small, dark crimson pools around her.

She had suffered massive blows to the head including one above the right ear and another directly to her face. When they found her, deep, gasping breaths escaped her lips. It was almost impossible to believe she was still alive. The poor woman died before medical help arrived. Even if medical professionals had arrived sooner it wouldn't have mattered. The injuries were too extensive for her to have lived.

When Allegan County investigators arrived, they found Mrs. Baldwin's 35-year-old son, Elton, standing nearby, staring blankly at the body of his mother. When asked what happened, he shrugged and said someone must have come in the house while he was outside doing chores and killed her.

According to Elton's story, he had gone out to do chores around 4:30 A.M. His mother called down that she would be up directly to fix breakfast. When he returned to the house an hour later all was quiet. That's when he discovered her on the floor. There was blood staining her pillow and he heard her gasping breaths. Terrified, he locked up the house and went to a neighbor for help.

Elton was not an immediate suspect. Indeed, on first inspection it looked like the home had been ransacked. Drawers had been opened and clothes thrown everywhere. Deputies believed someone had come in looking for money. Their suspicions, however, turned to Elton as the investigation continued.

As the investigation progressed, it seemed there was a possible connection between two major barn fires and Elton. The barns were on property also owned by the Whitney family. Elton was having issues with the Whitneys over money owed. He was suspected as the incendiary of those fires.

Investigators thought it particularly suspicious that Mrs. Baldwin had been attacked just days after the fires. They also considered Elton's behavior at the sight of his dying mother very suspect. His attitude was nonchalant and unaffected by her condition. Elton quickly became the main suspect in both cases.

With Sheriff Ferris tied up in the transition process, Deputy Sheriff Fred Parr took over the investigation. It was Deputies Fred Parr and Will Roda along with Prosecutor Hoffman who brought

Elton in for questioning. Their interrogation lasted into the morning hours.

According to an article in the March 5, 1909, edition of the *Muskegon Chronicle*, it was around 2:30 A.M. when Elton finally confessed. "I killed her. I was afraid that she would say I set fire to the barns."

He continued with his story, initially blaming his mother for the barn fires. "I didn't fire the barns; and I suspect mother did it; and I took the hatchet and hit her four times with it."

After further questioning he admitted to setting the barn fires as well. When asked why

Elton Baldwin.
Man who killed his own mother.

Kalamazoo Gazette, March 7, 1909

he would kill his mother in such a terrible way, he paused for a moment, then matter-of-fact responded, "It was a funny thing to do, wasn't it?"

Not long after that, the floodgates opened and he began revealing the details of his crime. Elton's mother discovered he had set the fires and told him she was going to tell the police. She was going to have him put in jail. Elton couldn't bear the thought of being locked up so he decided he had to "destroy her."

According to Deputy Sheriff Parr, as Elton told the sordid story he seemed completely void of emotion as though unaware of the horror of what he'd done. He was immediately arrested and locked in the Allegan County Jail. According to a March 6 article in the *Kalamazoo Gazette*, he had been "placed in an upper cell that is usually kept for women or insane persons."

Later that afternoon he asked the jail officers if he could go to the bank and withdraw some money. "I think I ought to bury her," is what he said. Of course, he was not given permission but acting

Sheriff Volney Ferris agreed to handle the transfer of money for Mrs. Baldwin's burial.

The next day Elton Baldwin pled guilty to the murder of his mother in the Allegan courthouse. Reports say that, throughout the proceedings, Elton continued to remain nonchalant, unemotional, as though he either didn't care or didn't understand the seriousness of the crime. In fact, at one point, he told his attorney he wanted proceedings over with as soon as possible. When asked why, his response was that he wanted to go hunting in the Upper Peninsula and the quicker he served his time in prison the sooner he could go up north.

On sentencing day, Elton stood before the judge. His demeanor remained calm and relaxed. After a scathing speech by the judge calling Elton Baldwin the lowest form of life, he sentenced him to life in Jackson Prison. It was then, and only then, Elton finally broke down, completely collapsing in the courtroom. He was dragged back to his cell where he remained until his transport to Jackson Prison.

According to records, during his entire time at Jackson, Elton received only one visitation. It happened more than thirty years after the trial. His visitors were two former acquaintances from Allegan. It was said to be the first and last bright moment in Elton's life.

Elton did not have friends at the prison. In fact, inmates stayed away from him. It seems they found the nature of Elton's crime too horrible, too unforgivable, even by their standards. He remained alone and isolated the remainder of his pathetic life.

As my thoughts returned to the present, I wondered if any of Elton Baldwin's energy might remain to haunt the prison. Hopefully we would collect evidence that might validate that possibility.

I turned my attention back to Lorena who was ending her series of questions in *the hole*. We moved to other cells on the top floor continuing the investigation.

Our eyes scanned the interior of one cell. Faded names and words were scrawled on the chipped walls. We tried to make out

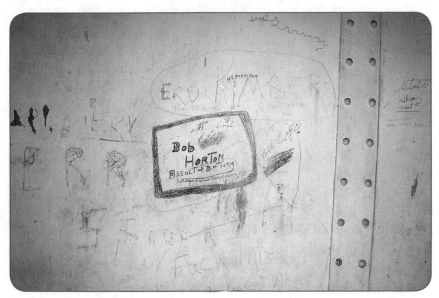

Graffiti tells the story of the prisoners' lives.

some of the names and words. One former prisoner named Eric wrote, "Damn, how'd this happen?"

Another name was Bob Horton, followed by "Assault & Battery."

Robert "Red" Ridder wrote, "Born to lose and I did."

Lorena and I became caught up in deciphering names and words scratched into the walls. Someone was in love with girl named Penny and hoped she loved him back. Another wrote, "100 and a half years in Jackson."

Each of the scrawled words and names marked layers of time and exposed the thoughts, prayers, anger and fear of real people locked behind these bars. Some of the words and names were too faded with time to be read. There was no way to know how many years the graffiti went back.

The remainder of our time on the third floor was uneventful, and we headed down to the level below us, turning right off the stairway. This route takes you past the historical plaque of Allegan County sheriffs and the row featuring some of their portraits. I glanced at the pictures, my eyes momentarily stopping on the portraits of Sheriffs Pratt, Grover and Stratton.

Courtesy of Old Allegan Jail Museum

(L) Benjamin Pratt, sheriff twice, between 1847 and 1857;
(R) Jacob Grover, sheriff from 1859 to 1861.

Benjamin Pratt was sheriff decades before the current jail museum was built, serving from 1847 to 1849 and again from 1853 to 1857. A great, white beard consumed his face, and his eyes stared out from the portrait with a blank, glazed expression.

Back in those early days, a sheriff's salary could not sustain a family so most held other jobs. In Benjamin Pratt's case he was the owner and manager of Allegan House, the town's stagecoach stop.

Next to the portrait of Pratt was Jacob Grover, sheriff from 1859 to 1861. He sported a beard to rival that of Sheriff Pratt's. I must admit the dark, intense eyes and stern expression was more than a little intimating. For a moment, Grover's eyes held me in an unsettled trance. I had seen eyes like that before and tried to remember where. Then it came to me. Charles Manson.

My eyes finally settled on the portrait of Joseph Stratton. He stared out with fathomless eyes. Whatever he was thinking at that moment lay hidden behind them. That was the kind of man Stratton was, an enigma. His deepest thoughts were a mystery with the answers known only to himself.

Stratton served as Allegan Sheriff from 1893 to 1896. At that time, the Allegan jail was standing not far from where the current jail museum is located. Joseph Stratton was a respected citizen of Allegan County. He was a dedicated, skilled lawman who served the county well but his term was not without controversy.

In 1894 a gang of masked bandits stopped a slow moving train. They robbed the passengers before taking off on horseback. Sheriff Stratton was notified by telegraph of the robbery. He and his deputies went off in search of the desperados. They eventually came upon a disreputable group of guys hovering around a campfire and held them. Several hours later, after some investigation, Stratton was convinced the men weren't involved and let them go. His search continued.

Joseph Stratton served as sheriff between 1893 and 1896. Suicide ended his life in 1916.

What Stratton didn't know is that because the train was also a mail train, a U.S. Federal Marshal and the well-known Pinkerton Detective Agency had gotten involved in the investigation. It is believed that Stratton, unknowingly, arrested the U.S. Marshal when he found the man nosing around the evidence.

To say this was a big mistake on Stratton's part is an understatement. The marshal was furious. Once released, he had Stratton along with his deputies arrested and jailed in Grand Rapids. The town of Allegan was shocked. The next day a group of the town's most well-known citizens boarded a train for Grand Rapids. There they immediately posted bail and released their lawmen. Stratton stood his ground throughout this ordeal, never blinking an eye or offering a comment on the surrounding events leading to his arrest.

The desperados were eventually captured. Some believed it was the good work of Sheriff Stratton that led to their arrest.

At the end of his term, Sheriff Stratton came into good fortune. In the summer of 1896, he was given more than $1,300 in reward money for the capture of a notorious Indiana train robber and the recovery of stolen money. Though others involved in the capture of the robber also tried to claim the reward, the courts awarded Stratton the full prize. He left office a relatively wealthy man.

For the next two decades Stratton remained a prominent and influential member of Allegan. He lived a seemingly happy life with his wife, son and daughter and kept busy tending his large farm. As he grew older, his energy began to drain. Those secretive eyes and unspoken thoughts took their toll. Deep depression slowly consumed him.

On a cool March afternoon in 1916, Stratton's wife and daughter returned to the house after doing outside chores to find Stratton on his bed with a revolver next to him and a bullet hole through his heart. The news made headlines across Michigan with a March 17, 1916, edition of the *Kalamazoo Gazette* reading, "Former Sheriff of Allegan Suicides. Suffers Nervous Breakdown."

Such a tragic end, I thought. Here was a well-respected man who appeared to have everything but, in the end, wealth and prestige had nothing to do with his inner demons.

Turning from the portraits, I joined Lorena in the back cellblock. Sitting on the hard metal of a lower bunk in one cell, I listened while she began another EVP session in the cell next to mine.

"Can you knock on the wall for us? I'm sure you did that to talk to each other." A few minutes passed in silence. Lorena continued, "Can you tell me why you're in here? Are you angry to have women in your cells?"

I added a few additional questions without response. Everything remained frustratingly quiet until I heard Lorena from the next cell. "I just had a crazy spike on my EMF."

I quickly entered and saw her staring at the EMF meter on the top bunk. There was pack of cigarettes inches away. She had left the cigarettes there as a gift for whatever spirits remained.

Lorena told me the spike hit when she reached to remove the cigarettes. It wasn't a minor fluctuation but a huge shot up to a full 45 milligauss. Normal EMF readings fall somewhere between 0 to 1. The sudden and brief 45 reading was incredible. I asked her to repeat the same movement, which she did several times. EMFs remained flat.

We rechecked levels throughout the cellblock, but no fluctuations were found. Returning to the cell, Lorena then began another series of questions.

"Did you like to smoke? Were you a smoker." She continued for several minutes but EMFs remained flat. The team would have to pay close attention during the review process to see if evidence had been recorded at the time of the spike.

We continued the investigation in other cells. I decided to call out the name of one Allegan's most notorious prisoners.[1]

His name was James. He was just 16 years old, a Boy Scout patrol leader and once a good student. No one suspected he was capable of such a horrific deed.

Two little girls, ages 11 and 12, were out picking wildflowers near their Holland, Michigan, home on an early April afternoon. The girls never came home. Their parents were frantic. Police and sheriff's department organized large search parties. Some reports claimed more than 500 people joined in the search.

They began on the quiet roadside where the children had last been seen. It wasn't long before a short trail of fallen wildflowers was found. They followed the wilted blooms which led them to a remote, rugged section of Macatawa Dunes near the shore of Lake Michigan. Discovered beneath mounds of fallen leaves were the lifeless bodies of the children.

To the horror of the families and community, the bodies were riddled with bullets. The suspect was identified almost immediately. His shocked and unbelieving mother reported to the authorities that she had found a note in her son's room. It read:

"Mom, I'm sorry but it was an accident. I tripped over a log and the gun went off a couple of times. I didn't mean to do it. When you read this, I will be on my way to Arizona and New Mexico. Keep your chin up. I'll be back. Don't do anything rash. Your loving son."[2]

---

1   We are withholding the last name and dates due to living descendant sensitivity

2   Taken from Schenectady Gazette

Not for a moment did the authorities believe it was an accident. Both girls had been shot in the head at close range. One girl had been shot five times, once directly between the eyes. The other girl shot seven times. A semi-automatic rifle doesn't unintentionally go off 12 times.

A .22 caliber semi-automatic rifle that was found hidden in the attic of his mother and stepfather's home was identified as the murder weapon. The hunt was on.

Newspapers across the country headlined the search for "The Boy Slayer." Within a few days he was picked up by the police in South Dakota. At first he resisted, saying they had made a mistake; he wasn't the person named James. After eight hours of interrogation, he gave in, finally admitting to the murders. According to South Dakota police, the youth showed absolutely no emotion or remorse when he confessed.

Upon hearing the news, an Allegan County Deputy Sheriff got in his car and drove 1,200 miles to South Dakota. He took James into custody and brought him to the Allegan County Jail where he remained throughout the court proceedings.

The youth was tried as an adult. During the trial, James' attorney claimed the young man was insane. Several witnesses confirmed his behavior had radically changed in the six months preceding the murders. Normally a quiet, polite young man, he became morose and erratic. His grades dropped. He shared morbid "blood curdling" thoughts including a growing curiosity about what it would be like to shoot someone.

Allegan County deputies confirmed James appeared uncaring, completely unemotional and unregretful about the deaths. Two psychiatrists interviewed him at length and brought conflicting testimony regarding his mental state. Both, however, shared a common belief that the youth did have abnormal personality patterns. James was convicted of Second Degree Murder and given a sentence of up to 40 years. It is unknown what happened to him after the conviction.

I called the name of James again, not knowing if he was still alive or dead, wondering if his confused, homicidal energies might

(L) Dawn and (R) Jessica had time to smile
while investigating the second floor dining room.

still remain. I whispered, "The person who killed the little girls …
is he here?" The only obvious answer was silence.

Eventually we moved to the cellblock on the opposite end of
the second floor. This is the area where the cells had been converted
to an old-time village of sorts, with each cell offering a peek into
nineteenth-century life. We continued the investigation.

Meanwhile Bev, Dawn and Jessica were conducting their
own investigation in the residence portion of the museum. Much
like Lorena and I, things had remained very quiet. EMF levels
remained relatively flat and no unexplained sounds or suspect
ghostly voices were heard.

This is very typical during investigations. We know there
are always stories from people talking about their crazy-active
ghost hunts. They had *feelings*, were touched or pushed, heard
disembodied voices, or saw shadowy apparitions dart from dark
corners. We cannot discount that possibility. The reality, however,
is these types of experiences are very, very rare. The vast majority of
actual paranormal investigations are quiet and uneventful.

Of course, just because an investigation appears uneventful,
does not mean something paranormal did not occur. Some of
the most paranormally active locations were identified through
evidence discovered after a quiet investigation.

Most experienced paranormal investigators are not discouraged when a hunt results in little experienced phenomena. This was the case for Bev, Dawn and Jessica. Though their time was uneventful, they were not discouraged.

After sessions in the upstairs residence and sitting room, the trio moved into the kitchen. This is where the sheriff's wife prepared prisoner meals. Elsie Runkel was one of the wives. Wife of Allegan Sheriff Walter Runkel, Elsie served as County Jail Matron for more than seven years. It was estimated she prepared and served over 24,000 meals per year. A challenging task no doubt but one she skillfully handled. It is thought Elsie's spirit might be one of those remaining at the residence.

The first thing Bev, Dawn and Jessica noticed were slight EMF level fluctuations generating around the large wooden table in the center of the room. The fluctuations were not major, just a few points, but still the group couldn't determine the cause.

The operating electrical appliances and outlets in the room were immediately suspected but it was determined they generated little if any EMF levels. The spikes grew higher near the center of the table. More unusual spikes were tracked to a gear bag that sat on a chair next to Bev. Nothing in the bag could have generated EMF. Besides, the bag had been with them throughout their investigation and no previous EMF spikes had occurred.

That's when Jessica began to consider another possibility. "What if your bag is in somebody's chair?"

"Let's try just the chair," Bev suggested as she moved her bag. Sure enough, with the gear bag removed, the EMF continued to inch upward from 0.4 to 0.5.

"Is that somebody's chair?" Jessica asked. EMF rose to 0.7.

"Ms. Elsie?" Dawn asked. "Are you sitting there now?" EMF went to 0.8.

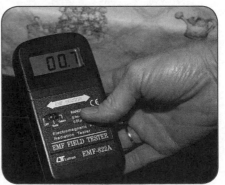

EMF spikes were
noticed in the kitchen.

The women shared brief glances. Could the spirit of Elsie Runkel be with them?

Bev began, "Are you getting ready to fix a meal, Elsie?"

Jessica continued, "Can you tell us what's one of your favorite meals?"

That's when the K2 hit again, its lights flashing rapidly. "Woah," Bev whispered. "What's going on?"

Their questions continued as EMF levels randomly fluctuated. Bev, Dawn and Jessica began to suspect the levels may come from a natural rather than supernatural cause since field variations didn't respond to specific questions.

They discovered the likely cause of the high EMFs when the furnace turned off and the heat stopped flowing from the registers. That's when the EMF levels immediately dropped to zero and remained there.

Though Dawn had checked levels at all the heat registers before with no EMF changes, there was likely something associated with the furnace running that affected the electromagnetic fields. Lorena and I would later confirm EMF levels did elevate when the furnace started.

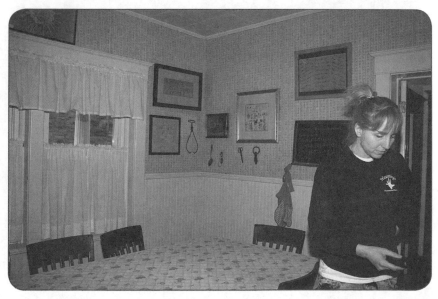

Dawn checks EMF levels.

It wasn't long after the furnace stopped that Dawn reported a sudden chill. Initially Jessica and Bev believed it was a draft from the windows felt once the heat had stopped. Bur Dawn insisted it was more than that. She was freezing cold.

Temperatures and EMF levels around her were normal, but Bev and Jessica were surprised to find her hands ice cold. It was then that Bev's camera battery completely drained.

Dawn scanned the room before saying, "If you want us to know who you are, you can tell us your name; and we'll be able to listen to the recorder later."

Several minutes later, the walkie-talkie crackled and Lorena's voice came in saying it was time to switch. Jessica confirmed, turned to pick up the K2 on the table and stopped. Its lights were flashing like crazy… and this time the furnace was not running.

The last portion of the evening was uneventful like most of the investigation. It was around 9:00 P.M. when we wrapped. Giving our thanks to the kind women from the historical society, we headed home for a good night's sleep.

Over the next couple of weeks, Lorena, Bev and I slowly went through our recorded material. Although nothing was found on photographs or video, we were surprised at the number of EVPs identified. For this story, we will focus on what we believe are the strongest pieces of evidence.

The first occurred during our initial tour. We had just left an area of the basement where food produce had originally been stored and were entering the section containing Native American artifacts. It was in the outer room where an EVP was captured, "Hope they got that." The voice sounded male and obviously didn't come from our all-female group. I wonder if there was something we missed in that basement?

The next occurred when I was upstairs, alone at the residence sitting in the room considered the children's playroom. I asked if there was a child in the room. After my question, "Did you get hurt here?" A hushed, drawn-out child's voice was heard. Simple but powerful in its possible meaning, "Mother."

Yet another EVP was recorded on the top floor of the jail in the section called solitary confinement. I had asked if Elton Baldwin, the man who axed his mother, was near. A quick "yes" was recorded. I continued my questions, asking if he had hit her four times in the head. Within a second a there was a clear response, "Crazy." This single word summed up what most people thought when the name Elton Baldwin came up, *crazy*.

It seems that Lorena and I may have received a few responses during the time we were reading the words and names etched in the cell walls. After Lorena spoke the name of Robert (Red), Ridder, a voice repeated, "Red."

I called out the name of Bob Horton and received another one word response, this one said "Horton."

Moments after Lorena called out the name of Douglas Tomkinson. A single word was recorded, "No!" It seems the spirit that remained wanted us to know he was not Douglas Tomkinson. Too bad he didn't say who he was.

The next EVP was captured in the hallway of the second floor cellblock, near the portraits of Allegan's former sheriffs. It said, "Sheriff Pratt." Though Sheriff Pratt served before the jail museum was built, we wonder if his spirit might remain attached to this portrait.

An additional EVP was collected on this cellblock, "Jules here." There is a member of the Hauntings Paranormal team called Jules, but she wasn't at this particular investigation. It could, however, be Julia (Jules) Ferris. Julia, who was frequently called Jules, was the wife of Sheriff Volney Ferris. Jules prepared and served meals much like other sheriffs' wives. Could it be a former prisoner at the jail telling others that the sheriff's wife had come to bring a meal.

For Lorena and I, one of the more eventful times during the investigation occurred on the second floor cellblock. Her EMF reader spiked to a full 45 as she reached for the pack of cigarettes on a bunk. Just after she recreated the same action, my digital recorder picked up these words, "I see that." There may well have been someone besides Lorena in that cell, and it seems like was craving just one more smoke.

For Dawn, Jessica and Bev, their unusual experiences occurred in the kitchen with the sudden EMF fluctuations and Dawn's sudden chill. The K2 hits seemed to be linked to the furnace operation; however, evidence may suggest there was possibly more to the fluctuations than the furnace.

The first EVP occurred shortly after the trio entered the kitchen. Dawn had quickly identified unusual EMF readings with Bev suggesting the fluctuations may be coming from the electrical outlets. It was around that time that Bev's digital recorder picked up an EVP that speaks over Dawn's voice. We had to listen to it a few times and can only make out a few words. We believe it says, "The [unknown word]'s correct."

The next recording occurred during the time they were asking questions of Elsie Runkel, wife of Sheriff Runkel. Jessica asked if it was difficult cooking for the inmates at the prison. Hauntings Paranormal's digital recorder picked up the voice of a male that said, "She could be bad." Was this ghostly voice referring to the well-loved Elsie? Perhaps her goodwill and kindness had a darker side.

An EVP was also recorded shortly after Dawn's reported chill. Jessica asked, "If you want us to know who you are, you can tell us your name ..."

Following that comes the word, "Ericka." As of this writing, we have not been able to connect an Ericka to the prison. Should we find a connection we will post the details in the Secret Room of our Web site.

Moments later, Lorena called in on the walkie-talkie indicating it was time to switch. As the women were getting their equipment together, the K2 hit again. After listening to the audio, a voice was recorded, "Get out."

Though our personal experiences were limited for this investigation, it seems the audio evidenced collected is compelling enough to suggest at least some of the stories surrounding the Allegan Jail Museum's haunting are true. Whether you're interested in its history or its haunting, we recommend coming to this fascinating place and see where some of the county's most well-known *desperados* once stayed.

About the Authors

Kathleen Tedsen and Beverlee Rydel

Kat and Bev continue their search into the world of the paranormal with their second book, *Haunted Travels of Michigan, Volume II*. This follows the success of their first, *Haunted Travels of Michigan* that received the 2009 IPPA Award for "Best Paranormal/Educational Book and Authors."

Over the past two years the authors have traveled more than 10,000 miles. They have been on scores of investigations to find ten of Michigan's most fascinating stories for their new book.

Kat and Bev are not new to writing. Since 1991 they have authored the *Michigan Vacation Guide* series. It was placed on the Secretary of State's "Read Michigan" list in 1995 and remains one of Michigan's most comprehensive publications on unique places to stay in the state.

With their new paranormal book series, the authors approach each investigation with a skeptics eye. To Bev and Kat it isn't just the haunting but the history of the location and lives of the people from the past that create the haunting.

The authors want to share their investigative experiences with the reader and take them into the ghost hunt. To accomplish this, each story contains a password that allows access to Secret Rooms on their Web site. In the Secret Room readers can see photographs, video and audio of evidence collected during the investigation and behind-the-scenes of the hunt.

Over the years Kat and Bev have been featured guests on numerous radio shows and television shows, including PBS TV's Michigan Magazine. They have also been guest speakers at various paranormal conferences. In addition, their speaking engagements include presentations at libraries, charitable events and historic locations across the state.

The authors began their paranormal journey as skeptics. Today they know that in many cases there is something out there that cannot be explained. Something paranormal.

They continue their search into the unknown.

Paranormal Investigative Teams

In our *Haunted Travels* book series, we frequently work with a paranormal team during an investigation. Over the years we have interviewed numerous paranormal groups. The teams we work with demonstrated a true commitment to the field of paranormal investigation. They consistently used sound methods and objective analysis in the collection, review and identification of paranormal evidence.

Each of these groups conduct investigations under controlled environments to accurately identify suspect paranormal evidence from natural sources. Each actively attempt to debunk/disprove suspect paranormal evidence and are serious in their efforts to help those in distress. None of the groups charge for their services.

We are very pleased to have worked with these reputable teams during the investigation phase of our stories. Let us briefly introduce them to you. They are listed in alphabetical order.

Hauntings Paranormal Research Society

Founder: Lorena Wygant

This team was recently formed in Michigan, but each member has extensive experience in the paranormal. Lorena has spent much of her life investigating the unknown and was a member of a TAPS affiliate while in Nevada. She has studied the paranormal from several well-known people including Lloyd Auerbach. Her co-founder Dawn has spent over fifteen years researching the unknown. They work with a highly experienced team.

Hauntings Paranormal uses some of the most modern technology during an investigation. Their cadre of equipment includes a DVR system and extensive collection of handheld video and audio equipment.

The group is very accurate when reviewing evidence and attempts to disprove what is collected. Lorena is certified as an EVP specialist and extreme care is used when labeling something an EVP.

Highland Ghost Hunters

Co-founders: Jennifer Marcus and Lisa Mann

Formed in October of 2005, Highland Ghost Hunters is led by two dedicated women, Jenny Marcus and Lisa Mann. They carefully screen and train all of their investigators to make sure investigations are handled efficiently and evidence review is

done properly. Together they create a friendly, trustworthy team that demonstrate the highest level of respect for individuals and commitment to each case they work. Highland Ghost Hunters are genuinely concerned about the people who need their help.

While all members of the Highland team help in equipment setup, Jenny and Lisa take the primary lead.

What impressed us the most with Highland is their dedicated, thorough analysis of audio, video and photographic material collected during investigations. They also use a very aggressive approach to debunking suspect evidence.

Mid Michigan Paranormal Investigators

Co-founders: Matthew and Melanie Moyer

Matthew and Melanie Moyer are the dedicated husband-and-wife team that lead Mid Michigan Paranormal Investigators. They are both experienced in conducting paranormal investigations and are committed to researching and finding explanations for ghostly phenomena.

During our investigations with Matt and Melanie, we were fascinated by some of the tools they used for investigation that includes the much-coveted thermo-imagers.

Mid Michigan Paranormal Investigators has built a reputation on honesty. The team goes out of their way to try and debunk something before calling it evidence. Matt and Melanie's team consists of seasoned investigators with extensive backgrounds in the paranormal as well as new, well-trained members.

The Upper Peninsula Paranormal Research Society

Founders: Tim Ellis

Tim Ellis leads this seasoned veteran group of paranormal investigators. They are a TAPS affiliate and one of the premier Mid West paranormal teams. They travel across the Upper Peninsula and Northern Michigan to find the truth and help those in need. With their tremendous amount of experience and knowledge, they host paranormal conferences and provide support to other teams.

Like the other groups we work with, they have a complete complement of equipment. In addition, the team has designed some of their own equipment in an attempt to improve evidence collection.

This dedicated group is very analytic and thorough in reviewing evidence. If there are any questions as to a piece of evidence, they don't use it.

What is a Ghost?

The simplest explanation… it is the remaining *energy* that exists after the physical body has died. Does that mean all of us will eventually become a ghost? The truth is no one really knows, though it seems unlikely.

The empirical law of physics says that energy can neither be created nor destroyed; it can only be transformed from one state to another. Everything on earth is made of energy. That includes us and, of course, our dog BoBo and our cat Priscilla, Queen of the Jungle and All Things Relevant.

Our physical bodies are a powerhouse of energy and our brains the *god of energy*. It controls our body, our thoughts, feelings, and beliefs. When our brain dies our body dies. Where does all this energy go?

Based on the principles of physics, the energy that created our physical body dissipates after our death, like a drop of water in the ocean. It moves to another state. For people of faith, the energy that is our essence, our soul, transforms to a greater existence.

Ghosts come to exist when the deceased's energy, or at least a portion of their energy, doesn't fully dissipate or transform. Its energy becomes trapped. This *trapped* energy is frequently connected to a traumatic incident, a strong emotion or memory, and its remaining energy the basis for a variety of paranormal activity.

Based on our more than 100 investigations, there does appear to be a relationship between paranormal phenomena and a past act of violence, despair, sadness, and/or love. On several occasions, this energy has attached itself to a home or an object that played an important part of the deceased person's life.

A common theory is that a person doesn't have to die at a location for his or her energy to exist there. It becomes attached to a location, or locations, and sometimes people in which the spirit energy finds some bond or connection.

Of course, if a ghost is truly a spirit energy, who can say with certainty their energy must be only in one location? We have conducted at least one investigation that involved both gravesite and home where valid EVPs (electronic voice phenomena) were recorded, both appearing to be responses from the same supposed spirit.

How long does the spirit energy remain? That is yet another unknown. Perhaps the answer is as simple as the strength of the energy and the reason for its strength. For example, an energy may remain strong to look after a loved one. Once it knows this individual is safe, the energy weakens and transitions. Certainly, based on recorded EVP, at least some ghost energies remain for hundreds of years.

Every year, there are thousands of people who report seeing dark, shadowy figures, human-shaped mists and other physical manifestations of people who cannot possibly be there. If closely studied, most of these reports can easily be dismissed as misperceptions, hallucinations and over-active imaginations.

In spite of that, there are a small percentage of reports that, even under study, cannot be explained or dismissed. It is this small percentage of unexplained sightings that drive us to learn more, to investigate and, once and for all, fully explain, validate or dismiss the existence of ghosts.

Paranormal Gear Bag

Latest Technology In Paranormal Investigation

There are several pieces of equipment that have become standard technology found in a paranormal investigator's gear bag. Still cameras, hand-held night vision video cameras, and audio recorders are among the most common. Others include thermo gauges, electro-magnetic field detectors, and motion detectors. Certainly the multi-camera nightvision DVR system is desired, though more expensive. Of course, if the investigator has a few extra thousand dollars, they'll pick up the coveted heat-signature camera thermo-imager.

Of all these, however, the single most important piece of equipment is the flashlight. Yes, that's right, the flashlight. Whether exploring the darkest recesses of some abandoned prison or even the back room of a haunted theater, the flashlight is the most critical piece of equipment to have in your hand. It is your lifeline to sanity and will steer you safely across broken floors or old, rickety stairways.

Recently, there has been a variety of new equipment introduced into the paranormal community. They are said to improve identification of paranormal phenomena. Some of this equipment does seem to hold promise others, however, are more *toys* than important pieces of technology to add to your paranormal gear bag. Though new equipment is popping up all the time, here a few that seem to be gaining popularity:

Frank's Box (i.e., The Ghost Box)

This device uses AM radio frequency to pick up random audio signals and generate white noise. The theory is that these random signals and white noise will allow spirits to create their own vocals through the receiver (talk through the box). Newer versions of this box tunes (scans) back and forth through various AM bands.

There are many obvious problems with this piece of equipment. First, and most important, it is irritating. It is constantly picking up small clips of actual AM radio broadcasts. The investigator is hearing white noise with broken, random words. More than a few minutes of this will lead anyone running for the quiet of some dark, creepy basement.

Second, it is too easy for someone to hear and interpret a random voice as being from a spirit when it is, in fact, just a piece of AM broadcast.

Third, the loud, static noise and random voices can contaminate or completely override other disembodied voices or sound phenomena. The contamination not only affects the room in which it's placed but also in surrounding rooms. The sound of the static and voices easily carry into other rooms.

Fourth, the theory of its design is questionable. How does a *spirit energy* know how to use these signals to generate its own words? Is there some direction manual on *the other side*? What made the developer of this device identify that spirits were even able to pull radio signals to create their own voice?

We do not use Frank's Box (The Ghost Box) on our investigations and do not consider results from Frank's Box as evidence of paranormal activity.

Full Spectrum Camera

Through a series of light-filtering, the full spectrum camera captures levels of light and images that go beyond the light spectrum our natural vision can detect. This allows images or shapes unseen or *hidden* in other light spectrums to become visible. There has been increased use of this camera system in recent investigations.

Though an interesting approach to identifying light variations unseen by the human eye, it does have its problems. In traditional photography it is difficult to identify a paranormal event because the picture captures just one brief moment in time. It is unknown what natural occurrences happened at the moment the picture was taken and, therefore, makes it very difficult to determine if the photographic anomaly is a result of natural causes or a true paranormal event. It becomes an even greater issue when using a full spectrum camera.

When going outside the visible light spectrum, it is incredibly difficult to determine the source of the anomaly because, obviously, the image captured was not seen. False positives are very likely misinterpreted by someone inexperienced in spectrum photographic analysis. We would suggest getting educated in full spectrum photography before attempting to use it to identify paranormal phenomena.

Geophone/Siesmic Motion Sensor

The geophone detects vibrations and flashes a series of LEDs that measure the intensity of the vibration. It may be useful in detecting footsteps or other vibrations that may not be noticed.

A good example of its use is in a case of an individual who believes his bed moves or shakes at night. A casual observer may not notice the bed shaking. However, the geophone would detect the movement.

Ion Generator

This is a piece of equipment that charges an area with electricity. In the paranormal community, it is believed ghosts will be drawn to this electrical energy in order to manifest. Recent testing does not seem to validate its use in investigations.

K-2 Meter

The K-2 meter is a simplified version of an electromagnetic field (EMF) detector. Instead of identifying EMF fields via numbers, it uses a series of LED lights to signal increasing levels of electromagnetic fields. A green light designates normal and red, the last light, signals very high EMF. In the paranormal community it is believed unusual spikes in electromagnetic fields can signify a spirit energy is near.

The K-2 has been found to be quirky and sometimes unreliable. The meter can signal high EMF in response to use of walkie-talkies, cell phones, TVs or other electronic equipment. Because of that, a response by one of these meters has to be looked at suspiciously. All electronic equipment should be tested with the K-2 and cell phones should be turned off during investigation.

What's nice about a K-2 is that EMFs can be monitored across a room. When you see the lights flashing, the investigator can quickly ring their tri-field meter or EMF detector to validate the spike.

We have used the K-2 on many of our investigations. During our Doherty Hotel investigation, the K-2 did dramatically respond to a series of EVP questions.

Ovilus

The Ovilus is said to translate EMF (Electro Magnetic Field) readings into numbers and then translate those numbers into words. This allegedly allows spirit energy or other entities to verbally communicate with the investigator.

We have seen/heard the Ovilus on investigations. The supposed words coming out are random and, very often, not clear. This opens the way to the individual investigator's interpretation.

As of this writing, the manual for use of the Ovilus indicates it is for entertainment purposes only. We're not certain how the developer identified what EMF levels create what numbers and how those numbers relate to words. To date, no logical reason for its translations methods have been given. We do not consider results from the Ovilus as paranormal evidence.

Zoom Stereo Audio Recorders

This a high-end, multi-mic digital stereo audio recorder. It is considered a surround-sound recorder because it is able to pick up lower decibel audio in a 360 degree pattern. The sound from this amazingly small audio recorder is excellent. It generates remarkably clear audio.

We have heard EVPs recorded using the Zoom H2 and a Tascam DR07 recorders and were surprised at the clarity compared with a traditional digital audio recorder. If you have extra cash, it's a good recorder to add to your gear bag.

Let's Look at the Evidence

Searching to find the truth about the paranormal is a non-stop quest for many people. Paranormal groups use all sorts of video and photo cameras, recorders and special lighting to try and gather evidence. Their equipment has become much more sophisticated.

Some paranormal investigators tell us they are scientific-based, though most have no formal education or advanced knowledge of scientific methodology.

What they really mean is they are technology-based investigators, using a variety of technology to record, analyze and identify a haunting. Technology-based investigators differ from others who use psychics, mediums or sensitives as a source of validation.

High-end equipment can be quite expensive. Some equipment, like the thermo-imaging camera, can cost thousands of dollars.

Why is so much money spent on this equipment? It allows investigators to find the truth and validate the existence of life beyond what we know and also for personal satisfaction. There is nothing more gratifying than collecting a genuine piece of solid evidence to validate the existence of the paranormal.

Collecting evidence is a source of pride in the paranormal community. It certainly is for us. We want to find meaning and justification for all the weekends spent away from family and friends.

With most teams, when evidence is found after an investigation it goes right up on their Web site, Facebook, MySpace or YouTube. The web is flooded with proof of the paranormal.

We have to ask ourselves how much of it is real, misunderstood or simply fake. Generally, it only takes a little common sense, a healthy dose of skepticism, and an understanding of the equipment being used to determine if something is actually evidence of the paranormal. Let's take a look at various types of evidence collected to develop a good understanding of what is and isn't genuine.

Photographic Evidence

Much of the evidence out there is photographic. Photos capture just a fraction of a second in time. Collecting something real in a photograph is very rare and most of the time we are simply misunderstanding what can cause abnormalities in pictures. Though a still camera seems so simple, many of us simply are not fully aware of how a camera works. We have included a collection of some common photo abnormalities at the end of the chapter. Most are not paranormal.

During our investigations, we have taken over 30,000 photos. In all those still images, we have only captured one photo we consider something paranormal (See Sample 1).

Sample 1: Valid photo evidence like this is rare.

Here are some things to consider when analyzing photographic evidence.

Orbs

We will begin with one of the most common… *orbs*. These are generally roundish. Most are slightly transparent while others may be more solid in appearance. They are frequently white though can also come in an array of colors. Many paranormal teams consider themselves experts in the study of orbs. We call them orbologists.

Unfortunately, nearly all orbs are really nothing. For the most part they are dust, insects, pollen, humidity and a result of reflected or refracted light from your camera's flash or other natural occurrences, like the sun.

It was in the mid 1990s that orbs were first considered evidence, about the same time first generation digital cameras became popular. Many believed that with this new, advanced technology they were able to pick up spirit energy (orbs) that were hard to capture in traditional 35mm film cameras. Of course, orbs were sometimes found in cameras that used traditional film, just not nearly as often.

Unfortunately, many less expensive digital cameras have reduced lens quality that create noise, or clutter, and are more likely to create orbs in the image. The vast majority of orbs are created when the camera's flash or other extraneous light bounces or reflects off unseen particles, moisture or insects in the air. This creates a transparent and/or glowing round circle in the photo (See Samples 2, 3).

During our investigations we use several photo cameras. One is an expensive, high-end camera. The others are point and shoot digitals that cost less than $500. The less expensive cameras always generate orbs. In fact, we lovingly refer to them as our "orb cameras."

Sample 2: Moisture orbs.

Many leaders in the paranormal community, such as Troy Taylor, lecture and write about the fallacy behind orbs. Yet, no matter what they say, orbologist continue to provide their expert knowledge on this subject.

Sample 3: Dust orbs.

Honestly, we are not sure the terms "expert" and "scientific" are appropriate when dealing with anything paranormal. Almost all of it is based in conjecture and theory rather than known, scientific methodology and facts. Some of the theories associated with ghosts and hauntings make sense while others are just wild theory.

Now, why do orbs have colors? Many orbologist Web sites go into great detail regarding the meaning of colors. They say one color means calm or serene while other colors means anger, love, evil, and so on. In reality, colored orbs are simply air particles absorbing color from their surroundings and transmitting that color in the picture.

In numerous photos we have taken containing colored orbs, with just a little review and common sense, we were able to identify the color of the orb with something else in the room or area. For example, orange, green and brown orbs are often captured outside. These colors are found in plants and trees.

There are actually genuine orbs, or balls of energy. Ball lightning is an example. These energy orbs can be seen with the naked eye and are a scientific reality. Because they are balls of energy, and spirits are believed to be an energy-based phenomena, we can't completely dismiss the idea that some energy orbs may actually represent real spirit manifestation. We will say that 99% of orbs are really nothing. Because of that, our Haunted Travels books will never include orbs as evidence. Sorry orbologists.

Enter the Matrix - Photos of Apparitions in the Window

Let's move on to that ghostly face or apparition in the window. We have seen many of these photos that, at first glance, appear genuine. While there may be some that are valid evidence, the photos we've seen and investigated have turned out to be the result of natural causes. You need to look at the surroundings inside and outside of the building.

The glass in windows, by its very nature, can easily pick up reflections. If there is a suspect paranormal image in the window, check to see what might be causing it. There could be other buildings, trees or even another investigator's reflection in the glass. A very common cause of window images is the sky. Clouds can easily look like a woman in white or that evil demon the photo captured.

It's not just outside reflections that can cause us to see an image in a window. We also need to know what is in the room. Is the suspicious image a chair, door or lamp?

What we are talking about is something called *matrixing*. Matrixing is seeing familiar things in random patterns and shapes. As children we would look up at a cloud and see a bunny, a bird or maybe Uncle Fred wearing a cowboy hat. That is the perfect example of matrixing and is a plague for inexperienced ghost hunters.

If a suspicious image is captured in a window, go back to the site at the same time of day and under similar weather conditions. Take several pictures of the same area, at the same and different angles. Take into consideration all possible interior/exterior causes. If you cannot go back to the building, it is best to dismiss the image.

We were at a reputedly haunted restaurant on an investigation a couple of years ago. One of the common, recurring paranormal occurrences was the apparition of a woman's face in an upstairs window. Naturally, during the investigation we took many photos and video of the window to see if we could capture the image.

To our great surprise, in a couple of photos we did see a face in the window. Upon inspection of the upstairs room, however, we quickly discovered our ghost person was a lampshade hanging from the ceiling. Again, we just want to emphasize the importance of knowing what is on both sides of that window before making a judgment (See Samples 4, 5).

Matrixing is another common cause of ghostly apparitions in mirrors. Aged mirrors are particular culprits of ghostly apparitions that aren't. As a mirror ages, its polished, dark metal base and glass can experience moisture leaks, fine cracks, chips, warping, and other natural wear that can create some very fascinating shapes that may appear to be faces.

Mirrors, just like windows, capture and reflect light from any variety of sources including the random flash from a still

Sample 4: Many people have seen a face in the
upper floor window of this restaurant.

Sample 5: The face is actually a lamp and a perfect example of matrixing.

camera, infra-red (IR) light, or flashlight. Even the position of a partner or placement of furniture can create a matrix effect in a photo.

Sample 6: The photographer swore he had captured a ghost dog in the cemetary.

Matrixing does not always appear in windows or mirrors but can occur anywhere, especially in the dark. That's why it is so important to know where team members are and to be aware of your surroundings (See Samples 6, 7).

Spectral Ectoplasm

Another commonly mistaken photo is one showing ectoplasm, which is believed to be a form of spirit energy. Though it may be a valid paranormal event, there are many non-paranormal things that can be its cause.

Sample 7: The ghost dog was actually the statue of an angel.

Cigarette smoke is a frequent cause. When analyzing a photo with suspect ectoplasm or strange mist in the picture, it is not uncommon to see an astray nearby or a cigarette in someone's hand. When we point this out, the person will swear no one was smoking in the room until we point out someone in the picture with a cigarette in their hand. The truth is, sometimes the obvious is overlooked.

Ecto can also be created during periods of high humidity and low-lying clouds/fog. Mist or streaks of light can occur with or without a flash if the aperture setting of the camera is slow. This can give you a very clear picture but cause any light source to streak (See Samples 8,9,10).

Blame the camera as well for that dark shadow frequently showing up in pictures. A weak flash, a finger partially obscuring a portion of the lens or even a camera strap will give off uneven lighting creating a dark shadow, mist or shadow person to appear (See Sample 11).

Sample 8: Smoke looks like ectoplasm.

Collecting Video Evidence

When filming an investigation, usually in very low light settings, many of the same things can occur as with photography. That orb traveling across the screen is probably a bug or dust. The size of the orb, as with a photo, depends on how close the dust, pollen or bug is to the lens.

Low light video, even with infra-red (IR) lighting, is grainy. Often shadows in a room appear to move or take shape. Be certain you are not falling into the matrix trap. IR can frequently cause a shadow person to appear all

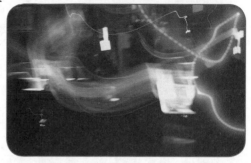

Sample 9: Slow shutter speeds cause streaks.

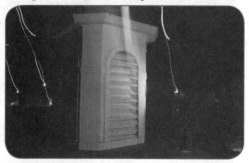

Sample 10: Street lights also cause streaks.

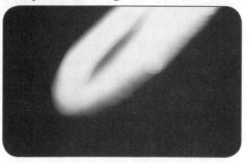

Sample 11: Camera strap.

by itself. A surge or fading of electrical or battery power can cause the IR to malfunction and create distortions.

Completely normal variations in lights and shadows appear in night vision video. The bright light shooting across the screen more often than not is the beam of a flashlight, headlights from a car coming through a window, or the glare of a light reflecting off a surface. As with all evidence review, it is really important to know where every team member or other people in the building are at all times.

A person can be standing out of camera view but reflect a shadow against a wall simply from an extraneous light source. Not long ago, a world famous celebrity died. A local news crew was shooting video for a TV piece in his former home. A spirit or shadow person was seen walking in a back room. It was all over the Internet. The shadow had a strong resemblance to the celebrity and looked so genuine. Turns out the shadow was cast by a TV crew member.

Collecting Audio Phenomena

One of the most common pieces of evidence collected today is electronic voice phenomena (EVP). A voice so low it's impossible or hard to hear with the human ear but is able to be captured on audio. These EVPs can be really good evidence. Again, there are a few things to remember.

We all know not to whisper during an EVP session. The person asking the questions always speaks in a loud clear voice. Unfortunately, others in the group frequently whisper to each other, even though they know they shouldn't. Those whispers frequently turn into an EVP a few days later.

Many times investigations are in old buildings where sound can easily travel through walls and even floors. People talking or walking on another floor or room can sound just like a ghost. Even outside street noise and voices can be caught on audio. We have heard EVPs that turned out to be a camera turning on, someone's stomach growling, or a furry critter scampering across the room. Always look for extraneous sources that could cause the noise.

Should someone cough or make a noise when moving, they need to clearly say what just happened. Even people with the best memory can't remember what was going on every second during an investigation. This becomes more apparent when the material collected may not be reviewed for several days or weeks.

If more than one audio recorder was recording when an EVP was captured, see if you can hear that noise or voice on the other recorders. Also, check any video camera that may have been filming the area. The movie may clear up any uncertain noises or voices.

Most often an EVP is recorded that seems pretty clear, but we still can't make out the words or other people don't seem to hear them at all. That is when we take the audio and run it through software to enhance the sound.

Manipulating audio can make the voices much clearer. If over adjusted the EVP begins to sound like chalk on a blackboard, just shrill squeaking and very mechanical. Only minor adjustments such as white noise elimination, volume, pitch and speed changes should be made. The key word here is "minor."

Electro Magnetic Field Evidence

Paranormal groups also use a variety of devices that pick up atmospheric or electrical changes in a room. The most common are Electro Magnetic Field (EMF) detectors including K2 (often spelled K II) meters. There are two parts to electric charge: the static electric field (which is constant and based on the total amount of electrical charge present) and the fluctuating magnetic field (which is based on the actual flow of electricity). Expensive EMF meters can read both, while the K2 only reads the magnetic field.

Most ghost hunters believe spirit manifestation to be a form of energy. When EMF meters detect a rise in energy levels it could represent such a manifestation. Some investigators believe the K2 meter is a way to communicate with spirits. When a spirit is asked a question, they will gather energy in an attempt to answer causing the LED to spike. These spikes can occur to represent yes, no or as affirmation to the question.

As with all equipment, we need to understand how EMF meters operate and what can trigger the device. Since they basically measure electric forces, there are many normal things that can change the electromagnetic field. Just a few potential causes arc cell phones, appliances, strong magnets, walkie-talkies and even solar flares. If you are holding the EMF meter, any sudden movement will cause the reading to jump.

Before using EMF meters, take baseline readings so you know when there is a significant spike. Keep in mind the most common causes for EMF increases is electrical wires, wall plugs, fuse boxes and old copper piping. If EMF is elevated in the middle of a long hall, along a ceiling or wall there is a good chance it is wiring.

How can we be sure evidence collected is good? There rarely is 100% certainty in proof of the paranormal. We don't take our experiences and evidence back to a lab for scientific testing or try to completely duplicate all outside elements that might impact what was collected.

With just a few key principles to live by, evaluating good and bad evidence is really very simple. Be objective at all times. Record or keep notes on what's going on to help jog your memory at a later date. Know where team members and others are at all times during an investigation. Realize that we are not perfect and the equipment used is not perfect, and understand what can cause abnormalities.

Finally, let's just use some good old common sense and not be so eager to call something paranormal evidence. When in doubt, throw it out. It's important to get rid of some of the nonsense found online today. We want to prove to ourselves and non-believers that there really are things we can not explain… something truly paranormal.

Ghost Hunting Terms

Learn the words, know the words, become the words...

Apparition

A spirit or energy that is visible to the human eye can be captured on video or in a photograph. Generally it has the shape resembling a human form, but may take the shape of an animal.

Battery Drain

This occurs when a fully charged battery is suddenly drained of power. This drain can be a result of explainable, natural causes. Unusually cold or hot temperatures rapidly reduce battery life. In some cases, however, it may identify the presence of an entity. The theory being a spirit, in order to manifest, draws energy from many sources. Batteries are one of those sources.

Cleansing Prayer

A prayer to cleanse any negative or residual energy that may attempt to attach itself to people during paranormal investigations. It is also the spiritual cleansing of a home to eliminate psychic disturbances or negative energies.

Cold Spots

A localized area where the temperature is noticeably colder (10 degrees or more). Applying the same theory mentioned in Battery Drain, it is believed entities draw energy in order to manifest. One of those sources is heat energy. This is said to create cold spots in an area of a room where an entity exists.

Deliverance

See Exorcism.

Demon/Demonic Presence

These are considered non-human, evil entities that are frequently hard to control. Often they are referred to as fallen angels. It is believed they may surface during use of an Ouija Board or through the practice of Black Magic.

People or families most frequently affected are found to be under extreme personal stress. It is believed the nonhuman entity takes advantage of people in such weakened psychological and emotional conditions.

Ectoplasm

A white-gray transparent substance often resembling a mist. It may materialize as a result of spiritual energy or psychic phenomenon.

Electronic Voice Phenomenon (EVP)

The voices of spirits or ghosts, speaking words at a decibel levels below the normal range of hearing. These disembodied voices can often be recorded on digital or tape audio recorders. Use of audio editing software may be used to enhance their clarity.

There are three generally accepted types of EVPs:

Class A means the recorded voice is clear enough for most people to understand without software enhancements. Capturing a Class A EVP is very rare.

Class B words are open to some interpretation. They can sometimes be as loud as Class A, but the words are mumbled and unclear.

Class C are the most common. These audio files are low decibel whispers or voices usually very difficult to understand. Audio enhancement is required to improve audibility.

Electro Magnetic Field (EMF)

An area with high levels of electronically charged objects. EMF is often the result of energy from a spirit or ghost. It may also be the result of electrical wiring, or machinery.

Entity

Used to refer to a spirit or ghost. It has a distinct existence but may not have a material form or body.

Exorcism

The practice of removing demons or evil spirits from the body of a person who has been possessed. It is often done by an exorcist, frequently clergy, involving prayer and religious acts. The person possessed is not considered evil, and the exorcism is looked at as a cure. During an exorcism the person being cured can become extremely violent.

Fear Cage

A room or area with extremely high EMF readings from excessive electrical wiring or equipment. Many people have strong adverse reactions when exposed to high EMF levels. Physical effects can include nausea, headaches, skin rashes, feelings of paranoia, dizziness, tingling sensations, delusions and hallucinations.

Ghosts

The image of dead people, often looking very much like themselves in appearance. Ghosts are most often seen in places they used to live or visit regularly, such as a loved one's home. They can also attach themselves to a possession they once owned. Frequently they are responsible for paranormal activity including cold spots, objects moving, apparitions and footsteps. These spirits can be both good and bad.

Haunting

A place, person or object that has repeated paranormal activity. These activities would include sightings of apparitions, voices, strange unexplained sounds and moving objects.

Infrared Light

A lighting and video recording system that goes beyond normal light waves to illuminate in total or near total darkness.

Infrared and Laser Thermometer

Used to measure the temperature of an object from a distance. Often they are called laser thermometers because a laser is used in aiming. Ambient thermometers will check surrounding air temperatures instead of a specific object. All assist paranormal investigators in detecting sudden drops in temperature, which may indicate the presence of an entity.

Intelligent Haunting

When a spirit or ghost is aware of its surrounding. Often they will respond to questions being asked or make noises such as footsteps, turning lights on and doors closing. In an intelligent haunting it is not uncommon for objects to move or be hidden. The spirit can take on traits of the living person with certain odors or smells from perfume, flowers, cigarettes, etc.

K-2 Meter

A new and supposedly advanced EMF detector that uses lights instead of a needle to detect energy levels. It can be used to communicate with the spirits by asking them to flash the light for yes/no answers.

Matrixing

A person's ability to see something familiar, most often in a photograph, from a series of complex colors or designs. The most common objects seen are a face or body. Extreme caution should be used when reviewing photographs that are dark or blurred to avoid this.

Medium

People with the ability to communicate with the dead. Physical mediums draw energies so their clients will hear or see sounds, knocks and images. Mental mediums will see, hear and sense the sounds. The spirit communicates through the medium.

Orb

A circular, translucent, light colored floating object that represents a source of energy. When a lot of orbs are seen it can mean the manifestation of a spirit. They are very rare. Generally, what many consider orbs are simply dust, bugs, pollen and other small articles suspended in the air. When the small object gets close to a camera lens it can appear large and translucent. Caution should be used when considering an orb as authentic.

Ouija Board

A flat surface with letters, numbers and symbols used to communicate with the dead. Normally, participants place their fingers on a movable object, a planchette, in the center of the board. It is moved across the surface and receives responses to their questions. Many believe they are dangerous and should be avoided. It is easy to release evil spirits or demons and become spiritually possessed.

Paranormal

A term used to describe something out of the ordinary that cannot be readily explained. The word itself does not necessarily mean something, someone, or some place is haunted.

Parapsychologist

A person who studies the paranormal, such as survival of a spirit after death. They use a variety of methodology and testing in their work including laboratory research and fieldwork.

Poltergeist

A spirit or ghost that actively moves objects. A few even speak and have distinct personalities. Generally they occur around a person and are thought to come about when the spirit experiences unusual rage or very strong emotions at the time of their death.

Psychic

A person with the ability to sense things that the average person cannot. This person is said to have extra-sensory perception. People with psychic abilities are often referred to as mediums and sensitives.

Residual Haunting

A haunting that is replayed in which there is no intelligent spirit or ghost. They are simply repeating some event, usually very traumatic or emotional over and over again. It is similar to watching a movie again and again. The same activities occur with little change.

Spirit

See Ghost.

Sometimes referred to as a ghost. The two words are often interchanged. It is simply thoughts and feelings of a person who has died. As with ghosts, spirits can be good and bad.

Supernatural

Very similar in meaning to paranormal but more directly related to the spiritual world. It refers to events, people and activities that cannot be explained using traditional concepts. Most notably a tern used for actions pertaining to spirits or ghosts.

Voice Phenomenon (VP)

Very similar to an Electronic Voice Phenomenon except it can be heard with the ear. To listen to a VP audio recorders are not needed. The voices of spirits or ghosts are speaking words at a decibel level high enough for the average person to hear.

Vortex

A spinning or whirling that is often captured on film. It is usually translucent and resembles a small tornado. Many believe it acts as a portal for spirits to come and go. Something that can be captured on film.

White Noise

The background hiss or static that is heard on a video recorder. Many times the white noise has to be filtered out in order to hear an EVP.

Haunted Travels
of Michigan

Volume II